MICHELLE KERR

Intuitive Impact

A Female Entrepreneur's Guide to Ditching The Doubts, Unlocking What's Already Inside You, and Creating An Aligned, Confident & Intuitive Impact On Your Terms

First published by Michelle Kerr 2021

Copyright © 2021 by Michelle Kerr

All rights reserved. No part of this publication may be reproduced, stored or transmitted in any form or by any means, electronic, mechanical, photocopying, recording, scanning, or otherwise without written permission from the publisher. It is illegal to copy this book, post it to a website, or distribute it by any other means without permission.

Michelle Kerr asserts the moral right to be identified as the author of this work.

Michelle Kerr has no responsibility for the persistence or accuracy of URLs for external or third-party Internet Websites referred to in this publication and does not guarantee that any content on such Websites is, or will remain, accurate or appropriate.

Designations used by companies to distinguish their products are often claimed as trademarks. All brand names and product names used in this book and on its cover are trade names, service marks, trademarks and registered trademarks of their respective owners. The publishers and the book are not associated with any product or vendor mentioned in this book. None of the companies referenced within the book have endorsed the book.

Michelle Kerr is the founder of Michelle Kerr Coaching. A coaching and community to support female industry leaders and business owners to grow their impact successfully from the inside out - without sacrificing their wellbeing, relationships or life goals.

You can connect with Michelle via:

Website: https://www.michellekerr.com.au
Instagram: @michelle.kerr
Email: hello@michellekerr.com.au

First edition

ISBN: 978-0-6451912-0-2

Editing by Caryn Pine

This book was professionally typeset on Reedsy.
Find out more at reedsy.com

Contents

Introduction   iv

I   Part 1 - Conquer the Past

1. The Masks We Wear — 3
2. What's Holding You Back? — 19
3. Rewrite Your Story — 47
4. You 2.0 — 66

II   Part 2 - Embrace the Present

5. Create Space for More — 79
6. Love Thyself — 93
7. What Do YOU Want?! — 107
8. Step Into Your Power — 121

III   Part 3 - Manifest the Future

9. Call It In — 141
10. Sustainable Supports — 160
11. Your Alignment Plan — 180
12. Intuitive Impact — 198
13. BONUS: Business Energy Archetype Quiz — 212

Introduction

I am not the expert, guru, hero, or saviour in your life.

For the majority of my life, I wanted to be needed by the people around me. When people needed me, relied on me or wanted me, I felt whole. It was part of my identity—being the one that people needed in their life for whatever reason. From trying to save the troubled boys in high school, to being a listening ear for friends and family, to becoming a counsellor where people sought me out for help.

But what I realised over the years, is that none of these people actually needed me to give any advice or feedback. They just needed me to listen and grant them the space to explore their own world. They needed to save themselves.

Because the reality is, the expert and saviour in your life—is *you*.

I can't make you change aspects of your life, or force advice onto you if you're not ready and willing to make the changes for yourself. I can't hover over you every day like a drone, making sure that you do the things you say you will or remind you about the goals you have. That, my friend, is up to you.

I am simply a guide, and by sharing the stories and insights that I've collected over the years, I hope to support you to realise that everything you've ever needed is already inside of you.

By simply picking up this book, I know that some part of you is ready to claim back your power and make changes in your business and life. I know that you're ready to stop letting fear, doubt and comparison hold you back from putting yourself and your gifts out there. I know that you're ready to show up more powerfully for yourself and your business so you can shine your light in a bigger way. And I know you're ready to become unwavering and attract the impact and income that you deserve.

Many times (and more often than not) change is surrounded by pain. It could be the pain of holding yourself back, the pain of failed expectations, the pain of letting people down, the pain of untapped potential or the pain of grief and loss.

Pain in its many forms can often jolt us awake in life and become the catalyst for us to choose differently moving forward. So many of my turning points, mindset up-levels and powerful choices have come from moments of feeling like I'm at rock bottom. A few that I will share throughout this book.

When you find yourself in the depths of darkness, grief or helplessness it can be hard to see where the light will come from. But like the cycles of the day, darkness is always followed by light. What I've found is that the light doesn't come from someone else, the light comes from inside of you. When it's ready to emerge and when you're ready to grasp onto it, the light burns brighter and brighter, guiding the way and lighting the path towards all of the things you want.

Turning inward and exploring the depths of your internal world isn't easy. It can be damn uncomfortable, and even traumatic. As a drug and alcohol counsellor, I saw the impacts of people who weren't able to go within. They would escape and numb out through substances to avoid the reality of their thoughts and emotions. Oftentimes, it was far easier to let themselves be seen as a drug user than to face how they really saw themselves. This book isn't about delving into your childhood experiences or processing anything that you're not ready to explore. But it is about bringing back your sense of power, worthiness and self-belief so that you can move through any of the stuck-ness you've been sitting in and begin shining that big, beautiful beam of light inside of you.

Throughout our time together, I'll lovingly guide you through three core phases to stepping into a more confident, aligned and intuitive version of yourself and your business.

1. *Conquer The Past* - In order to be able to make effective change and bring all of your desires into reality, you need to firstly adjust your relationship with your past. Ultimately, your past is what has got you to this exact moment of reading these words and without all of the mess and magnificence, you wouldn't be who you are right now. Even if that person is not the version of you that you want to be...it's the version that lays the foundation to step into your next level. This section isn't about forgetting your past, pretending it never happened, or putting a positive veil over all the things you wish never happened. It's about learning to stop letting your past control you and dictate your thoughts, feelings and actions now and into the future. It's about learning to embrace what you've experienced and see it all for what it is, so that you can free yourself from the hold and forge forward in creating new experiences that will one day become part of your history.

2. *Embrace The Present* – While it can sound pretty profound, the reality is that the only moment you really have is right now. That can feel both scary and liberating, but it also means that you have the power to choose how you show up in every moment. Sure, there'll be moments that pass by fleetingly, there'll be wasted moments, there'll be inevitable painful moments, and there'll be life changing glorious moments. But how all of the little present moments add up is what begins to form your reality and that's where you have the opportunity to choose. Will you choose love over fear? Will you choose belief over doubt? Will you choose self-love over sacrifice? Will you choose resilience over defeat? This section is all about empowering you to get comfortable in the present moment, so you can begin to make active changes to how you show up for yourself and your business every day.

3. *Manifest The Future* – The future isn't some far off dream or 'one day wish' unless you continue to let it be that way. The truth is that every day you're having thoughts, feeling emotions, and taking actions that are intricately paving your path forward. You may not see it that way right now, but this will be part of your journey inward and the liberation that can be found from owning your reality. The things that you want in your business and life are available to you when you align yourself with them more intimately and begin taking the small, inspired actions towards them.

As I sit here writing this during my holiday in Byron Bay, with a sunlit balcony and stunning view of the lighthouse (the most easterly point of Australia)...I am reminded of my mission and message.

I *am* the lighthouse. I am here to stand firm and guide you on your journey back home to yourself. By shining my light and sharing my brilliance, I support you to also stay the course and do the work that you're here to do.

I do this through combining my years of psychology knowledge and experience, lessons learnt from running a seven figure skincare brand, and supporting/coaching hundreds of women through my counselling and coaching to create their ideal business and life.

Thank you for choosing to take this journey with me and honouring yourself in this way. I'm excited to share my stories and insights with you, and I trust that this book will serve as an inspirational and informative guide as you step into showing up more powerfully for yourself and your business—and claiming your Intuitive Impact.

I

Part 1 - Conquer the Past

1

The Masks We Wear

'Muuuuuuum! Come and be my customer!' I shouted out across the house. I was barely eight years old and I'd just put the finishing touches on my latest business venture.

This time it was a fancy restaurant serving up my plastic food toys. I would make my mum and brother sit down and choose their meals from the menu, so I could indulge in running my fully fledged restaurant from the lounge room. Hilarious to me now, because my cooking skills are less than stellar.

Over the next couple of years, I engaged in numerous 'play' businesses that were often sparked by the toys/gifts I received. They included 'Shellz Soaps' where I sold soaps from a soap making kit, nail design with my range of nail polishes, a book store selling my parents' collection of books and of course a six month period where I was a stay at home mum with my new Baby Born doll pretending the garage was my house.

What was apparent from an early age, was my imagination and motivation to run my own business. I loved the idea of bringing my own ideas and creations to life and having people be interested in what I had to offer them.

My dad started a business when I was young, so I grew up around business and used to love visiting his office and playing with the invoice pad and cash register. I was always destined to end up running my own business—but then…I grew up.

Fast forward into my high school years and I became a part of the societal system of the 'work hard at school, go to university, get a good job, retire' mentality. There was nothing taught at school that fostered my entrepreneurial spirit and everything became focused on what university you could get into.

When I was nominated as Senior School Captain (the school's elected spokesperson and female leader) in my final year, the pressure to perform only became more important as I was representing the school image. By that time, I'd fallen in love with psychology and despite knowing there was a set path ahead of 'work hard, go to university, get a job' for me there was also an additional step before the 'retire' part—a burning goal to run my own psychology practice by thirty years old.

But little did I know, there would be a lot of shedding of expectations, writing my own rules, and removal of masks along the way that would lead me onto a slightly different path…

The Masks We Wear

What if I told you that you were wearing a number of masks in your life? What would you think? Maybe you would laugh it off and think I'm ridiculous for suggesting such a thing, or maybe you would have a deeper knowing that it was true.

As we create our reality each day, we go about our lives conforming to rules and social expectations of what to think, feel and act. We're told directly or indirectly what is appropriate and what is taboo, strange, illegal or immoral.

Over time we learn to fit into the molds of society and this is where we begin to don our masks. Different faces, attitudes and behaviours for different situations.

The problem with this is we can get so lost behind the masks that we wear, that we forget to show up as our true selves—without any mask at all.

The Collective

Whether you realise it or not, our society or the 'collective' dictates a large amount of what is considered normal and appropriate. Different cultures, religions, political parties, and sport supporters all have their own rules and social norms that dictate behaviour within that group—and ultimately a person's life. We're governed by rules and laws, kept in line by enforcement agencies, and raised in certain ways by our parents.

What many fail to realise for the majority or entirety of their lives, is that this is all a façade. It's a creation of order by other humans, with chains of authority and income levels that separate people into particular groups. Sometimes you're placed into a group that you don't want to be part of—such as: unemployed, homeless, incarcerated or terminally ill—and might take on norms or behaviours that society comes to know (and expect) of these groups.

The good news is that you get to choose your reality. You get to choose what behaviours and 'group think' you take on board for yourself, and how you ultimately want to show up in your life.

I'm not saying you can show up to work naked, break into a shop and steal some stuff or start skipping on your taxes. But for many of the things that society tells us we should or shouldn't do because of the mold we 'fit' into, you have the choice to take it or reject it.

In order to have a more intuitive impact, it's time to start challenging the collective. It's time to start thinking about what it is that you truly want and the kind of life you want to lead—and get ready to rise up to claim it for yourself.

The Roles We Play

Have you ever had moments where you feel like you're living someone else's life? Or moments where you wonder why or who you're really doing it all for? I definitely have. As a perfectionist growing up, I was all about making others happy and proud of me. I worked hard in school so my parents would think I was smart and loveable. I stayed in jobs that were beneath me because I thought I had to 'work my way up.'

I took on countless responsibilities and loaded my schedule with multiple jobs, study and business ideas so that people would see me as successful and driven. It wasn't until years later, as you'll see in this book, that I actually stopped and asked myself, 'What do you want?!'

I knew what I didn't want...I didn't want to have to 'prove' myself, I didn't want my adrenals to be on fire, I didn't want to miss family events and be too busy to see friends for months and I didn't want to miss out on the life that was right infront of me—my twenties! All because I was striving for external validation and success. I realized that it wouldn't matter what I did with my time, I would still be loved and valued by the people that matter. And that's when I committed to stop doing what I thought I *should* be doing, and started doing what I *wanted* to be doing. It wasn't long after that my podcast and coaching was born—the work that I needed to be doing, not only for all of you, but also for me.

We play many different roles throughout our lifetime. Daughter, friend, mother, partner, business owner, football supporter...and each of the different roles we play requires different aspects of our personality or different ways in which we show up. You might not act the same in your business or workplace as you would when you're at a bar with the girls, or at the local kids sport event. Again, we tend to adapt our personalities and our behaviour depending on the environment and situation.

There's nothing wrong with being in these roles or changing your behaviour across roles...but where it can become problematic from a soul and authenticity perspective is when you lose your sense of self in the process. When you play along with what everyone else expects of you, and forget what things would look like if they were how *you* wanted. Perhaps you wouldn't volunteer for the school carnival, or resist putting your kids in daycare, or hold back on how you feel with your friends.

It's important to see what roles we play in the first place. Many people go through life and don't really think about what they do or why they do it. So this isn't about stepping away from everything in your life, but it's about making sure it's serving you and allowing your true self to shine through. That all the things you're doing are ultimately making you happy...or whether there's some role adjustments or replacements that need to take place.

When I started putting more of my own needs first and was honest about how I wanted to show up in my personal and professional life, I felt huge shifts that allowed me to step into a new way of both being and doing, and feel *good* about the process and the results.

Women in Society

It's hard to talk about roles and masks in society without talking about how being a woman effects this. Historically, women have been seen as homemakers and not worthy of things like voting, running businesses or pursuing their dreams. As this has slowly evolved and women have started rising up and demanding equality, some expectations of women have adjusted and others have remained. Especially as mothers, there is an underlying expectation and pressure in society for women to effectively care for their children and also more commonly these days to contribute financially.

Many women I speak to feel the stretch to manage their children and family life, while also trying to run their business or be present in their job, and it often feels like there's not enough hours in the day. It's worthwhile thinking about how gender roles and expectations play out in your life, and whether you feel like there is an imbalance with the responsibilities placed on your shoulders.

A popular term that has been adopted by many women lately

is that of the 'mental load'. This refers to the list of tasks, responsibilities, deadlines etc. that accumulate in a woman's brain. Of course this can be an issue for men too, but it is commonly being associated with the burden and expectations placed on women's shoulders to be the primary caretaker, cleaner, cook and manager of the household. Things like remembering to pick up medication, new school socks, send out that work email, put three versions of dinner on the table for fussy eaters, book the vet appointment, pick up some bananas on the way to work—and all of the seemingly small little tasks that get done in the background but that pile up in a woman's brain making for a heavy load.

As we see a wave of women starting their own businesses and working from home, there is suddenly far more opportunity for women to make money while also caring for their children. But this also increases the list of responsibilities and tasks to manage, if you're expected to maintain the majority of household tasks *while* also managing a business.

Like with everything, there needs to be a balance (or as close as we can get to this often cringy word), and we can't do it all... even though we'd like to think we can! I truly believe with the right supports, systems and strategies, women can successfully grow their businesses while also growing their families and there doesn't need to be a 'choice' between the two. Perhaps that means certain sacrifices, and letting go of guilt or shame around some of those 'societal expectations' of what it means to be a mother. Like asking for help, getting childcare support or sharing more of the load with your partner where relevant.

As dynamics change and women are called to maintain jobs, provide financially or step into higher level positions, it's more important than ever to be making sure that your work actually *works* for you. That it's not taking you away from what you really want to be doing in the world or to settle with something because right now you can't see your potential for more or be supported by others to step into it.

The Women Before Us

My grandma on one side of my family is ninety-six this year and my pa on the other side of my family is ninety-four. Something that I think about often is the life and number of changes they've been through. Born in the 1920s, they've been part of wars, the advances in technology, the turn of a new century, the internet and more. Their generation has probably experienced the most significant growth in human evolution and society than any other generation will.

I often think about what the people before me have been through in their lives—especially the women—and how the choices they made and the suffering they endured has allowed me to be where I am today. Without my grandparents fighting in wars, living through periods of poverty, raising children and supporting the progression of our society I wouldn't be in a position now where I can vote, work and raise a family, earn a living from my laptop, travel the world effortlessly and share my voice with thousands around the world.

Your mother sacrificed her body and perhaps aspects of her life to bring you into the world and support you to flourish. She likely woke up every day with you on her mind and put your needs before her own. Just like my grandma did for her children, my mum did for me, and I will do for my children.

As I look to start my own family, I can reflect on some of the hardships and sacrifices that my own mother went through as a single mum with more empathy and understanding than I did at the time. I can see all of the ways that I'm in the position I am now, with the opportunities that I have created for myself, because of the choices that my parents and grandparents made.

Even if you don't have a positive relationship with your parents or grandparents, or have experiences that you're unable to forgive, there may be a way that you can see now as you go through this journey of growth on how it has served you—even if it's shown you what *not* to do. Maybe you can reflect on all of the women and men outside of your own family who have sacrificed, endured, fought, advocated and invested in the progression of your society or country so that you can do the things you're doing now. The things that may now seem so basic or expected, but were once never an option.

The women before you, and the men supporting them, have carved out our history and allowed us to be able to step fully into our creative dreams today. Their sacrifices have contributed to our achievements, and we are currently doing the same for our future children and grandchildren. By sharing your voice, advocating for change and equality, standing in your power and having an impact with your gifts—you pave the way for others to do the same and more in the future just like our parents and grandparents have done for us. What an amazing and special consideration.

There's still some way to go towards equality and peace around the world, but every day we have the opportunity to contribute to strengthening our future and having more autonomy over the direction of our lives, so we can follow the paths that those before us have helped to pave.

Bro Marketing

Over the past few years, the online world of business has expanded significantly. When I first started dabbling in websites, you needed to understand complicated coding; now I can build a drag-and-drop website in a weekend. As technology and software advances, it means that more opportunities become available to us in the online world and more people are able to take advantage of making a living online. The issue that can come with that is that online business and marketing strategies are largely unregulated.

The development of online business—particularly in the service space—has typically been dominated by white men who found a way to monetize their skills and teach others to get particular results. As software and technology has improved, there has been a flocking to the online space due to its promises of passive income and high ticket opportunities.

The online coaching and consulting space has seen huge growth over the past five years because almost anyone can enter this industry and choose to teach/support others. The issue that is becoming more and more obvious, is the saturation of 'bro marketing' which loosely refers to the sleezy sales tactics, false urgency, manipulation, privilege, and other marketing strategies being used and taught. People are beginning to awaken to these tactics, but it's often after investing a small fortune into a well-constructed marketing approach and seeing little gain or results.

When I entered the online business world of coaching and information products, I was also drawn into this facade of big promises and fancy possibilities. I even taught aspects of it in my own coaching because that was what I'd been shown to work.

But as time went on, I felt more and more uncomfortable with what I was seeing online and could see the cult-like characteristics of it. I watched a Netflix documentary late last year that explored a popular cult and couldn't help but feel sick from all of the similarities that I was seeing in the online business world. Bringing vulnerable people into a sense of community, asking them to invest heavily to show their commitment, using mindset blocks as a scapegoat for poor results or lack of privilege, needing people to move through the ranks (and invest more) to get more exclusive access to the 'leader' and creating dependency on the need for someone else to give you the answers.

That was when I really started asking myself how I wanted to show up online and how I could run my business and services in a way that maintained integrity, authenticity, transparency and trust—the bro marketing wasn't for me.

The reason I've included this section here is because it forms part of the false illusions that we can buy into on our way to our goals. Perhaps you've invested in coaches or programs in the past and felt like you have been duped. I know I have. But the purpose of this book is to firstly let you know that it's okay if there's been some missteps along your business journey, where you've trusted others more than you've trusted yourself. And secondly that you now get to choose how it is that you want to show up in your business and create success on your own terms.

Forget What You've Been Told...

'Mum, how did we get here?' I asked staring out the car window at the ripe age of seven.

'Where?' she asked.

'Earth,' I replied, staring at all the cement and rocks that had been used to build the bridges we were passing on our road trip, wondering where all of those resources had come from as well.

My mum said that I would always ask deep philosophical questions like that and she never really knew how to respond. I've always pondered existence, how everything came to be and how everything has got to where it is now. Although I may have questions that can't be answered simply, what this perspective has given me is the ability to step back and see things as separate to myself. It's helped me with letting go of my ego, with my sense of gratitude, and with making decisions about the kind of life and legacy I want to have.

My partner, Chris, has never been one to accept the status quo. He questions everything and stands up against anything that doesn't align with his values, morals or goals. He doesn't let other people's opinions, rules or perceptions hold him back from achieving what he sets his mind to. He is the one who showed me that it's ok to think differently, to stand up for what I believe in, to question the way things are 'done' and to pave my own way and to feel aligned in all that I do. He is the most resilient, dedicated and inspiring person I know and has taught me so much about life, love and leadership over our nine years together.

We only get one life. Whether you believe in life after death, the afterlife or multiple lives. Right now, in this incarnation of you— there is only one shot.

So as we begin this journey of turning inward, aligning and rising up together, I want you to forget everything you've been told. I want you to wipe the slate clean and know that from this day forward, you get to honour your needs and claim the business and life that you know you deserve and are capable of creating.

What's Your Business Energy Archetype?

As I started writing this book, I began thinking about what kind of person my reader was. What kind of wonderful soul would gravitate to this book and find it at the perfect time? I knew that my readers may be grappling with burnout, trying to manage business and family, feeling out of alignment, struggling to show up online and like they just don't fit the traditional mold of the entrepreneurship persona being flaunted for years. In a nutshell, my reader was exactly like me.

I started thinking about a fun way to describe and identify my readers and ideal clients, and began to see them as a range of archetypes that had different energies and values depending on what's important to them. That's when I conceptualised my Business Energy Archetypes. These are five different archetypes that are based on your energetic flow and the primary way that you share your value with the world.

The Hustler – You're a natural go-getter and have always been known for your strong work ethic and ability to make your goals a reality. When you decide on something in your business, you're quick to take action and get it done. People admire you for the consistent progress you make and the dedication you have to creating your desired results.

Unfortunately, that can often mean that you neglect other aspects of your life such as self care, relationships or fun. You may find yourself in periods of burnout after prolonged work output and require periods of rest or re-evaluation as you realise that you've over extended yourself.

The Rebel – You like to do things your way and find it difficult to follow specific rules, steps or pathways instilled by marketing gurus or celebrity entrepreneurs. You believe there a multiple ways to reach your goals and that there is no set criteria that you need to follow, other than listening to your own gut.

You prefer to position yourself as an outlier who does things differently in business and life, embracing your unique personality and ideas so you can showcase them to the world. You like to experiment and try new things, offer things that other people haven't considered, and blaze your own path to success.

The Intuitive – You use your gut and inner voice as your main directive when making decisions in business and life. You're a master at shutting out the judgement, opinions and advice of others and turning inward to decipher what it is that feels best for you. You base your business decisions on what feels good for you and feels like an energetic match.

You're tuned into other people's energies and can often absorb what others are feeling just by being in their presence. This can be both a blessing and a curse, requiring you to be able to detach from energies that aren't yours to hold. When you harness this energy you're able to lean into fully trusting and believing in your own capability and ideas, releasing into divine timing and flow to bring all of your goals to life.

The Creative – Your primary motivation in life is creating art in its many forms and sharing your creative bliss with the world. You may find marketing and selling a challenge, because your priority and energy source comes from being a maker/designer /artist/healer. If you could simply create things and have them sell themselves, you would be in your element. Being in your genius zone fuels your energy and you are easily depleted when you feel forced to undertake tasks that pull you away from your creative pursuits.

You prefer to be recognised for your creations and wait for opportunities to come your way, rather than impose yourself on others—but when not implemented correctly it can lead to scattered income. You communicate, connect and share yourself through your creations and are fulfilled by knowing that others value you and your work.

The Warrior – You use your story and lived experiences as fuel to guide and support others. You often move through peaks and troughs as you navigate your triggers, yet serve as an inspiration to others who have experienced trauma, discrimination or mental health struggles. Authentically sharing your story fuels your energy, and when you feel like you are hiding your truth or shamed for your beautiful vulnerability it can deplete you.

You provide a source of hope for others to be more than their past, their appearance, their limitations or their inner battles, and show the world that by embracing all parts of yourself and sharing vulnerably you can achieve great things.

To identify your unique Business Energy Archetype, take my fun and quick free quiz at the back of this book in Chapter 13.

Intuitive Insights

1. *What masks are you wearing in your life? Which ones feel comfortable and which ones no longer fit?*
2. *How have you let particular 'groups' or roles hold you back and limit your beliefs about your potential? E.g. – low income means unable to chase dreams?*
3. *How has society, gender stereotypes, and the expectations of others impacted how you've lived your life up until now? Which of these do you want to release?*
4. *When you remove the titles of daughter, mother, friend, business owner, etc.—what is it that's underneath? Who are you when you remove the superficial societal 'masks'?*
5. *How can you begin to embrace your business energy archetype and give yourself permission to do business in a new way?*

2

What's Holding You Back?

'We're getting a divorce.' My mum and dad looked at me from across the outside wooden table. I was only about eight years old at the time, so of course I didn't really understand what was happening...other than being told my family wasn't going to be living as a family anymore.

I can remember taking the news as maturely as possible at the time, but as the months passed and my dad had moved out, I remember asking my mum 'When will dad be coming back?'

He wasn't coming back, and as I grew up and learnt more about life and love, I knew that this was the best decision for them and for our family. My parent's divorce was probably as amicable as they come and I was incredibly lucky to have what I'd call a 'positive' experience of divorce. I spent plenty of time with them both and they were always supportive of each other.

But as I started working on some of my own blocks as an adult, I realised that I may have internalised some beliefs about myself back on that day at eight years old that I no longer needed to hold onto.

When you ask yourself 'When was the first time I felt like I wasn't enough?' What springs to mind for you? For me, it was the day at that table. As I explored this, I realised I'd let my parents' divorce mean that I wasn't enough.

I wasn't enough to keep them together.

I wasn't enough to keep them happy.

I wasn't enough to be the reason they kept trying.

And in the later years as they navigated their new lives as single parents, I wasn't enough to stand out and be seen.

I filled the 'not-enoughness' with perfectionism and working hard. I was getting A+++s in grade five, started my first job at fifteen, strived hard in all of my subjects and was Senior School Captain. By twenty, I was working three part time jobs while studying a full time Bachelor of Psychology Degree (which I also ended up fast-tracking over summer). By twenty-five I was working full time as a Counsellor, studying a full time Masters of Counselling Degree and running my new skincare start-up with my partner, Chris.

I'd always got attention and praise for standing out in this way, and being an overachiever became part of my identity. I was 'enough' when I was doing *more* than enough.

I thrived off the comments like 'I don't know how you do it,' 'You're amazing,' 'Where do you find the time/the motivation/the drive?'

By my mid-twenties everything I did was in the pursuit of advancing my psychology career and my fast-growing skincare brand. I wanted to be the #girlboss crushing it like I imagined as a little girl playing shop with her toys.

Until I crashed.

By 2016, our skincare business had gone far beyond a fun idea I had in my bedroom a few years earlier, and was beginning to far exceed our expectations. Everything looked good on paper...multiple six figure years, global contracts, products in huge retail stores. But behind the scenes I was struggling with anxiety, terrified of making *any* mistakes to the point of OCD (Obsessive Compulsive Disorder), in case it showed I was, in fact, not enough. I was neglecting things that I enjoyed in pursuit of more money, and on the not-so-good end of an adrenal fatigue diagnosis.

I remember being acutely aware that my mindset, energy management and mental health in this business would be the thing that could break us. That despite all of our success and hard work, my mindset and attitude had the power to unravel it all. It was at that point I realised that this pursuit to prove to myself and others that I was enough, that I 'had what it takes,' that I could 'have it all'...was holding me back from the exact results I wanted.

I was forcing myself to be the Hustler Energy Archetype, by telling myself that my worth and success came from how much work I did and how hard I tried to create results. I wanted everyone around me to see how dedicated and passionate I was about creating business success, that any moment of rest or non-work activities left me feeling lazy and uncommitted. Many business owners and entrepreneurs can easily sustain this outpouring of passionate energy. My partner Chris is a perfect example of this. He can work ten hour days, seven days a week and never get tired of putting consistent energy into generating ideas and income. I admire him for that and it's what helped us to create so much success with our business in such a short period of time.

But I've learnt over the years of trying to fit the mold of the 'never give up/do whatever it takes' expectation of entrepreneurs, that it's just not the way I work best. I ended up like many who force themselves to be Hustlers, and I burnt out. I lost my passion for my business because it was taking so much from me in terms of my wellbeing and relationships, which I valued more than success and money. My primary Business Energy Archetype is the Creative, which means I'm in my flow and recharging my energy when I'm achieving results through creative expression. Coming up with ideas for new products/services, designing web pages or graphics, producing video content and podcasts. When I'm sharing creative works from my heart for others to be able to take value from, it lights me up and creates results for me—both tangible and intangible.

It's taken me years to realise that there is more than one way of creating success and managing your energy in business. I'm finally feeling grounded and safe to work in these alternative ways that support my wellbeing and energy management, allowing me to give and serve from a better place—while supporting others to do the same.

Perhaps you're starting to realise that you've been forcing yourself to work in a way that doesn't suit you? Perhaps you've been thinking that the traditional ways we're told to run our businesses, just isn't vibing with you? Perhaps you've only realised it since opening this book?

Either way, I'm glad that you're here and that I can be someone to guide you through embracing your own system of energy management and output in your business, so that you can create results on your terms and in your own unique way.

But first, we need to explore what's been holding you back

and what needs to shift for you to feel more at home in yourself and your business...

When Did You Decide To Stop Believing?

Like most of us, there was likely a time in your life when you deciding to stop believing in yourself and your ability to achieve your goals. It may have been a subconscious moment or it may have been a moment that clearly sticks out in your mind.

Maybe you believe in yourself on the surface and make fabulous steps to achieve your goals, but then when it comes to the crux of it you end up flaking, self-sabotaging or retreating back to your comfort zone. When you're attempting new things and putting yourself out there in new ways, it's only natural to fear the outcomes and wonder if you really have what it takes to pull this off.

But the reality is that in order to chase your big dreams, you need to start with enough belief to take the inspired action and then continue to build your belief as you take more inspired action. You can't always start off with the level of belief that you would have at the end of achieving your goal, but you can start with enough belief to take the first step.

Belief builds...an aspiring singer may not have the full belief that they're going to be a worldwide phenomenon when they decide to write their first song, but they have the belief that they can turn their words into art and share their message—and let that be enough to take the first step.

So how can you muster up the belief to take the first step towards your current goal? How can you re-frame whatever it was that made you stop believing, and see it in a new light. Or perhaps even use it as fuel?

The Blocks In The Path

Everyone experiences blocks along the path when they're taking a journey towards something they want. These might be small setbacks or big setbacks, but one of the things that makes all the difference between those who go on to achieve their goals and those who don't is *resilience.*

Having resilience means that you're able to 'bounce back' from setbacks, rejection, hearing no, making mistakes, or being disappointed and not let it mean something is fundamentally 'wrong' with you.

In business, resilience is paramount for success because if you give up at the first sight of trouble or challenge, then you won't experience any success. There are so many successful writers, actors, singers, scientists, activists and more who chose resilience in the face of rejection. Many who were told they weren't good enough, that their work wouldn't be published, that they'd never make it...but they chose not to give up and are now achieving incredible things. Women like Oprah, J. K. Rowling and Jennifer Lopez.

Resilience is built in a few ways, but initially it involves not taking feedback or criticism personally. When I look at the people in my own life who demonstrate resilience, they continue to push forward with their goals and belief, despite what anyone says or thinks about them. When you permit feedback or criticism to mean something about you as a person it can chip away at your self confidence and is often the reason people choose to give up and walk away. For example, if someone says your presentation skills need work you would separate that from meaning anything about who you are as a person and focus on improving your skills in presenting. Sometimes it just comes down to doing something a different way, or having a different person come across your work.

Another part of resilience is having strong problem solving abilities and the fortitude to try again. Did you ever receive a complex puzzle or riddle when you were growing up and become frustrated because you couldn't solve it? You knew there was an answer or solution to it, but you either gave up or continued trying until you solved it. The same is true in real life. We all encounter problems and set backs in business and life, but those who choose to believe there is a solution and keep trying are often the ones who succeed in the long run.

Business Blocks

When you feel unable to take courageous action in your business, or in anything for that matter, I believe it comes down to one or more of the following business blocks:

1. *Limiting Beliefs and Old Stories*
2. *Fear and Self-Doubt*
3. *Your Business Survival Mode – Ingrained and Unhelpful Coping Strategies*
4. *Leaky Boundaries/Priorities*
5. *Unrealistic Goals and Expectations*

Limiting Beliefs and Old Stories

As we grow up, we're exposed to different situations, lessons, beliefs, and directions from others that ultimately form our own personal beliefs about ourselves. We begin to form stories about how capable (or incapable) we are and allow our mind to believe these stories and prevent us from taking action.

Your thoughts create your reality.

This is a significant mindset shift that many people will never make within their lifetime. It may take some time to sink in, but once it does it will create a whole new level of empowerment and control over what you manifest in your business and life.

This notion has been shared by coaches, authors and entrepreneurs and refers to the understanding that our thoughts and internal view of the world, transpires to create our reality and outcomes.

The theory proposes that your thoughts about a situation/experience, trigger an emotional response, which then triggers a behaviour/action, which then directly impacts the outcome or result that you achieve or are faced with.

I conceptualised this theory in a diagram called The Mindset Funnel, which I will cover in a future chapter, but it demonstrates the flow of how our thoughts, emotions and actions can ultimately have an impact on how our lives unfold. Meaning that you can play a vital role at dictating your internal and external experience of life.

Fear and Self-Doubt

One of the biggest mindset blocks is fear and the associated self-doubt. We are all wired to protect and preserve ourselves and fear pops up as an alert when we feel that our safety or security (also known as your comfort zone) is at risk.

I believe there are seven key fears that control people's thoughts and behaviour and are key areas that hold people back:

1. **Fear of Failure** - At the root of the fear of failure is the concern that you will be judged, shamed, embarrassed, and rejected. And when you're considering doing something that you love or means so much to you, the fear of being judged or rejected can hurt 5x as much and make us not even want to take the risk. But think about it, would you rather try something and it not work out, but that you learn and grow from the experience, or do absolutely nothing and stay in the same place as you are now? In order to push through this fear, you need to change the way you look at failure. Making mistakes, having something not work out like you'd hoped, or causing something to completely crash and burn can all be seen as learnings. Every single business owner, and every person for that matter, has made mistakes or failed with ideas. I've made so many mistakes in business, but the thing is, how would I know any different if I didn't make those mistakes?

2. **Fear of Rejection** - The fear of rejection is the concern that your actions, words, efforts, passions, even just your existence will not be well-received by others and you will be ignored, ridiculed, discarded or let down. The feeling of being ridiculed, not good enough or ignored outweighs the risk of taking a chance and seeing what happens.

   In order to push through this fear, the key is to start being ok with hearing 'no' or hearing crickets. So many successful people, have heard no so many times and not let that bring them down. You've probably seen stories about Oprah or J.K.Rowling and how many rejections they faced before getting that resounding yes that catapulted their career. Learning to hear so-called 'rejection' and being able to separate it from who you are as a person is critical in combating this fear.

3. **Fear of Uncertainty** - We have processes and systems in place to predict and plan our future to some extent, but at the very core of it, nothing is promised and nothing is certain to us. And that completely terrifies people.

   Focus on letting go of your control and expectations about specific outcomes. People with this fear love future planning, so try to let go of planning every little detail and practise becoming comfortable with letting things play out.

4. **Fear of Being Alone** - We live in a world now where we are always connected and always busy. Even when we have the opportunities to have some alone time, we are usually on our phones, watching tv, or distracting ourselves with something. This fear is often linked to relationships,

but I'm talking about the fear of being alone with your thoughts, your emotions, yourself. People can fear this and not even realise it because they jump straight into distraction mode with social media or tv, or they quickly think of another thing to add to the to-do list to stay busy and away from their internal world.

My tip here is to start creating space for yourself, and by that I mean quiet alone time with no distractions. Play some instrumental music, close your eyes and just allow whatever comes up to be. You'll be amazed at the shifts, ideas or healing that can take place when you give your body and mind some space. It will also support you to feel more comfortable, confident, and worthy in yourself in times when you are alone.

5. **Fear of Missing Out** - People with this fear hate to be left out of things, miss opportunities or not be a part of the action or trend. The problem with this fear and how it can be holding you back is that it drives you to be a part of everything. In business you might want to branch out into ten or more different revenue streams or have a foot in copious baskets because you've read that its what you need to be doing to enhance your business. The problem here is that wanting to do everything and be everywhere can work against you and soon become confusing and overwhelming for you, your customers and the people in your life.

To push through this fear, there needs to be some work around self-love and self-care. Working on your self-love and acknowledging that you are enough, that you are important, that you are capable of success—without going to that party or drinking that special coffee. I also recommend getting clear again on your goals and purpose—what it is that you actually want to achieve and how can you work towards this by selecting some key actions or tasks.

6. **Fear of Being Seen** - The fear of being seen refers to a concern around putting your face out into the world, speaking your truth, having a voice, putting your name to things, public speaking, or exposing yourself. The fear here is that by putting yourself out there, you open yourself up to judgement, criticism, embarrassment, failure and rejection—and that is all then reflective of you as a person. But the reality is, that none of this feedback or outcomes are reflective of who you are and don't determine your worth.

   The way to push through this fear is to just do it. Write a list of the things that you would do if you had full confidence and no concern for what others would think. Then look at your list and see which points you can start to implement. If they seem too much for you, how can you back track a little bit and make it easier to proceed.

7. **Fear of Success** - This is a tricky fear and often an subconscious one, because on the surface all business owners want to be successful and achieve their goals. This fear can show up in people who have past limiting beliefs or money stories that 'money makes you arrogant,' 'rich people only care about themselves,' 'you don't need money to be happy'…and this can cause you to self-sabotage your success. It can also show up for people

who fear up-leveling and potentially stepping away from family members or friends who are at a certain level, concerned that their loved ones won't see them the same or relationships will suffer due to their success.

Letting go of what people you care about will think of you is key to moving through this fear. Forging your own path and rewriting the limiting beliefs of parents, friends, partners and so on, will help you to create success on your terms in a way that feels aligned. Get clear on what success means for you and that you get to define how your life looks when you get to that place.

Business Survival Modes

Our survival response is commonly known as the fight or flight response, and refers to our subconscious reaction when we are faced with a perceived threat or our survival is at risk. We either instinctively 'fight' the threat, or take 'flight' and run away from the threat.

During our evolution, these risks have been substantial such as protecting ourselves from dangerous animals or other humans. However these days, those kind of threats aren't as common and many of our perceived threats have become 'irrational' in nature...also known as irrational fears.

We feel fear over a situation, and instinctively our brain feels like our survival is at risk so our survival response kicks in. We then participate in behaviours based on our survival response and *fight* the stressor head on, *flee* the stressor or the third more recent addition: *freeze* up.

The 4 Business Survival Modes:
1. Fight
2. Flight
3. Freeze
4. Combination: Frazzle

1. Fight Mode – The Workaholic/Hustler

- You work tirelessly on building and growing your business but often to your own detriment.
- You'll often be up early, stay up late, and sacrifice time with friends or family to work on your business.
- You spend countless hours doing 'all the things' but often aren't doing the right things in the right order and don't achieve your desired results.
- You're constantly 'fighting' for business success.

1. Flight Mode – The Avoider/Doubter

- You experience fear and doubt when it comes to building or growing your business, some of which may be subconscious.
- You feel like you don't have the internal or external resources to 'fight' or achieve desired results in your business.
- You have a tendency to avoid working on your business when life gets in the way or when things become too difficult or challenging.

- As a result, you make little progress with your business and lack a consistent plan to achieve your desired results.

1. **Freeze Mode – The Procrastinator/Perfectionist**

- You are passionate about building and growing your business but there are times when it paralyses you from taking action when it counts.
- You become easily overwhelmed, 'choked up' or stuck in inaction unless things can look/feel perfect.
- You move slowly on tasks and goals and struggle to make key decisions efficiently.
- You'll often find yourself doing procrastinating on business tasks by filling your time with other things and therefore struggle to achieve your desired results.

1. **Frazzle Mode – The Rusher/Tinkerer**

- You're a mixture of all three modes depending on the situation and your perceived level of competence to respond to a stressor or task.
- You're often rushing between tasks and thrive off last-minute deadlines that force you to focus and not get too stuck in your head.
- You often appear overwhelmed and 'frazzled' due to managing so many tasks and competing demands at once.
- You have bursts of momentum where you knuckle down and achieve results, combined with periods of avoidance or procrastination that makes it difficult to capitalise on your momentum.

The beauty of knowing your Business Survival Mode and common response to business stressors or fear, is that you can begin to notice these thoughts or behaviours when they appear and can replace them with more constructive thoughts and behaviours.

You begin to respond rather than react...

Reacting – mostly subconscious, automatic thoughts, emotions or actions to a trigger or perceived threat.

Responding – creating the awareness and space to recognise the trigger or perceived threat and *choose* how you respond.

Ideally, you want to be able to respond to business situations rather than react, so you can enhance your level of control over the situation and reduce the impact that it has on your stress levels and business progress.

How to switch out of your Business Survival Mode:

1. **Awareness**—*(My business survival mode is frazzled. I know that I can often sway between working too hard to avoiding/shutting down depending on the trigger and how I internalise it. I begin noticing my common reactions to specific situations in my business.)*
2. **Brainstorm alternative positive coping strategies / responses**—*(I make note of more positive ways I can manage my reactions – such as plan out my week with intention, practice meditation, avoid multitasking or being interrupted, create boundaries around my working hours, make time for my wellbeing etc.)*
3. **Challenge your automatic thoughts, feelings or**

behaviours when they occur—*(I become mindful of when my BSM is being triggered and practice 'catching it' rather than just seeing it as the way I am.)*

4. **Practice adopting your more positive coping responses instead**—*(Once I catch myself in acting out my BSM, I mindfully lean on my more positive coping strategies and work out which one I need most in that moment and respond accordingly.)*

Leaky Boundaries

Another common reason that people get in their own way or hold themselves back in business is by having leaking boundaries or priorities.

Boundaries refer to the clear rules, limits or agreements that you have with yourself or others about how you will/wont spend your time, will/won't be treated, will/won't tolerate etc.

Priorities refer to the things in life that you most value and align with and therefore find yourself spending the majority of your time, effort and money on.

If your **boundaries** are 'leaky' it might mean that you commonly sacrifice your own needs or wants at the expense of others needs or wants. For example – you might say yes to things when you want to say no, you might spend the day with your children instead of on your business because you feel 'guilty', you might put your partner's career and goals before your own, you might accept treatment from others that are unacceptable because you're not confident to share your voice.

If your **priorities** are 'leaky' it might mean that you put low level tasks or other people's priorities before you own, and may not even know what your priorities/values are. For example—you might put your children first because everyone has told you that being a mother is more important than anything else in your life, you might dip into your savings for a new car for your partner when you really wanted to spend it on a holiday, you might sacrifice your health/wellbeing at the expense of hustling in your business.

To have solid boundaries, it's important to be clear on your non-negotiables. *What are you no longer willing to tolerate? Where have you been leaking energy, time or money for others and not yourself?*

You may not always know your boundaries until one has been crossed, but then it's important to take note of where you feel a boundary has been violated. You can then have a conversation with yourself (or the person who has crossed your boundary) to determine how to prevent this from happening again.

To have solid priorities, it's important to be clear on what you really value. Often a good sign of what you value most, is where you spend the bulk or your time/money. For me it's family, learning/personal growth, business building and-self care. *What are your top three values/priorities in life? Where do you spend the majority of your money and why? What do you wish you could have in your life that you're currently neglecting?*

When you know your priorities you can begin to align with them and integrate them into your week as a non-negotiable, and ensure that you're always working and living in accordance with your highest values. That's when confidence and success breeds.

Unrealistic Goals & Expectations

When you have an expectation about something, you have a preconceived belief that a particular outcome will occur and often 'expect' it to happen as you planned. If this expectation isn't met, it can often leave you feeling disheartened, incapable or embarrassed.

Here are my six strategies for creating goals that feel realistic and being able to manage your expectations around how your goals play out:

1. **Build the solid foundations first**

    As business owners one of the important considerations is building solid foundations for your business to grow from. Similar to building a house, you need a planning blueprint, sturdy base and frames before you can add all the walls, pretty paint and furniture.

    When it comes to business, these solid foundations include things like the following:

- Clear business vision and plans for what you're going to sell, how you're going to sell it and who you're going to sell it to.
- Systems in place to attract and convert clients in both organic and automated ways.
- Software that removes the manual/repetitive tasks and allows a streamlined & clear client journey.
- Supportive people, mentors and environment to support you on your chosen path

- Channels to connect with your audience and provide them with value.
- Investment in your own wellbeing, self care, education and needs so that you can continue to grow your business without burning out.

So how do you focus on the foundations?
A big part of moving through this book is to get many of these foundations in place from the get-go. You're working on getting a clear idea of what your main business offerings will be, how to create a scalable systems around your offers, attracting your ideal clients in an aligned way, and then allowing these processes to create more time for yourself and less work.

A helpful reminder: when working on a task, ask yourself, '*Is this directly going to help build my income or impact today?*' If not, it probably isn't a key foundational task that needs your attention.

1. **Allow for consistent, sequential growth**
   No business is an overnight success. Building a business requires consistency, patience and commitment to planting the seeds of growth over time and allowing your actions to build momentum like the snowball effect. Even the businesses that appear to have shown up overnight and have huge success, are most likely not the owner's first business. The owner usually has a string of successes, failures, lessons, mentors and community that they've

leveraged in their current business to get it to where it is. Every small action that you take—every social media post, every blog article, every email, every behind the scenes task—helps to create a cohesive brand for your business and build your authority and credibility with your audience

So how do you focus on sequential growth?
Continue to visualise that every little step forward is another step towards building momentum for your brand, and that overtime these micro commitments will add up and position your personal brand for bigger and bigger growth.

I also like to imagine it like planting seeds. We plant the initial seeds, water and nurture them consistently and create an environment for growth and then we eventually see the flowers or fruits bloom

2. **Effort is required for mastery**
Just like a business doesn't have success overnight, it also doesn't have success without any effort. Get rich quick schemes, 'easy' routes or shortcuts are no way to build a successful and sustainable business. So we need to appreciate that in order to master a task or goal, we need to exert a level of effort. Effort might include ongoing learning, ongoing output and commitment to showing up, ongoing mistakes or setbacks that you continue to overcome. But, just because effort is required in business it doesn't mean it has to feel *hard.* You get to decide how you feel about the tasks in your business, and whether

you choose to delegate the things that don't light you up. A key to maximising effort in your business, is to do tasks in a way that can be leveraged down the track. How can you create systems, automations, delegations, workflows etc, so that you put the effort in to begin with but then over time the effort multiplies and creates growth without you having to be continuously exerting yourself?

So how can you focus your efforts?
Understanding that in order to achieve a particular expected output, you need to provide it with input. We all need to commit to our goals and put in the effort to learn, practice and master them so that we can see the fruits of our labour. However, always be considering how your upfront effort can be capitalised on and replicated for the future. Expectations often go unmet when you haven't committed to putting the required time and effort into something, and then you're unable to get the desired results.

3. **Turbulence and setbacks are necessary**
   Just like effort is essential to master a skill or goal, so is turbulence or 'setbacks'. If someone is never challenged, never makes mistakes or never feels like they're pushing their limits it's probably because they're staying within their comfort zone and not able to access the true learning opportunities that come from mistakes. If you have perfectionist tendencies, this can often be a tough one because you're motivated to get everything perfect the first time around. Sometimes this leads to inaction because you'd rather take no action than risk being seen

as making a mistake or not 'good enough'. The shift in mindset here is to embrace mistakes and messy action as being cornerstone to your growth and helping you to pivot and redirect.

So how do you focus on embracing turbulence?
Continue to push through feelings of fear or self-doubt and take small actions in a way that feels somewhat comfortable. Over time, your confidence will grow and you'll be able to take slightly bigger actions or risks.

Every year, I choose a word of the year. Over past years I've chosen words like Courage and Growth. It's meant that every time I feel fear or self-doubt, I remind myself to take courageous action anyway. I challenge myself to dive in, knowing that I might make a mistake or it might not be perfect, but I can always improve as I learn and grow. What word could you focus on this year?

4. **Decide fast, detach fast**
   Making decisions is a big part of running a business. It's often a big shift for people who have left corporate roles, as many of the decisions are made by managers or CEOS—now it's largely up to you.
   That's why it's important to tone up your decisiveness and be able to make decisions effectively and efficiently. One of the best ways to make decisions faster is being clear on your business vision, goals and client journey.
   When you embrace the power of 'one thing' and have one clear service that you sell to one clear ideal client and one clear strategy to sell that service (how I recommend

starting out your business offering)—decision making becomes super simple.

When you're no longer stretched across a million problems, service options, software and content pillars, you can ask yourself a simple question with each decision: 'Does this support my *one thing* vision?'—YES or NO?

For example, if I was approached to do a workshop on wellbeing for men in the trade industry, it's a one second NO because despite money and exposure it could bring to me, it has no relevance to my services or the audience I work with and therefore becomes a distraction from my goal.

So how to focus on decisiveness?
Measure your decisions against the following two questions:
Does this support my 'one thing' vision?
Does this directly increase my impact or income today?

Just like you want to be able to back yourself with the decisions you make and not be stuck in a cloud of indecisiveness, you also want to be able to detach from the outcomes/expectations of your decisions and move into a space of flow and surrender.

What does flow and surrender mean exactly? It means being able to let go of how your decision plays out and being able to surrender your expectations to whatever outcomes takes place. This also means that you're less likely to place your worth or ability onto outcomes, so you can remain in a state of flow with what manifests and then be able to reflect and adjust accordingly.

So how to focus on detachment?
Practice detaching from everyday situations and outcomes, such as consciously surrendering to situations like busy traffic, things not being delivered on time, people not responding to you or no one engaging with your content.

As you get better and better at detaching, you can encourage this state of flow and surrender across more and more things that you do so that you are less likely to hold onto unrealistic expectations or make negative outcomes mean something personal about you.

5. **Find the 'Goldilocks' for desired outcomes**
   Expectations can be similar to making goals, where we aim to achieve a certain outcome but it's not always known whether it will be achieved. Just like goals, you want to find a balance between expecting 'too much' and not 'expecting enough.'
   The Goldilocks Principle plays into this by finding your 'just right' expectations, where you're satisfied and grateful if your expectations are met but are also detached and unwavering if they're not met.
   This requires you to believe in yourself and your outcomes enough to not sell yourself short, but also not expecting so much of yourself that it becomes more than likely that it will be hard to achieve.
   The way that I manage my own expectations so that I can stretch and challenge myself, but also make space for

'less than ideal' results, is by using the good, great and amazing method for setting expectations/goals:

Good Goal – a very achievable outcome that would be the bare minimum ideal outcome
Great Goal – an achievable, realistic but fantastic outcome
Amazing Goal – an almost unrealistic, oh my gosh this would be so amazing outcome

Example – Clients per month:

Good Goal – three clients
Great Goal – six clients
Amazing Goal – twelve clients

What would your goals look like if you set it up similar to above?

It's Not About Letting Go, It's About Leaning In

An important distinction as you move through the 'Conquer The Past' section of this book, is that it's not about letting go of your past...it's about leaning into it. We often hear about letting go of past experiences, beliefs or traumas and that we must have a forgive and forget attitude if we're to release the grasp that the past has on us. But what if conquering your past actually meant *embracing* it? What if it meant leaning into all of the shadows, challenges, messy and uncomfortable times rather than running from them?

Your past is such a huge part of what has got you to this point, so you don't want to simply forget it ever existed...but instead acknowledge it for how it's got you this far. And if your Business Energy Archetype is The Warrior, you'll come to learn how embracing your story and sharing your triumphs and vulnerability with your audience is actually your superpower to more impact and income.

There are so many moments in my past that I wish I could flush down the toilet and pretend never existed. So many face-palm moments or memories that rise up right before I'm about to fall asleep and make me cringe into my pillow. Things like messing up important wholesale orders with the wrong stock, being too selfish with my actions that impacted others, or getting way too drunk at parties in my early twenties and not acting myself.

But as I've learnt more about the power of our thoughts and also the power that resides in our past, I've been able to lean into those uncomfortable moments and see that I wasn't the person that I am now. Hindsight is 20/20 and I can lean into the fact that many of the moments I wished didn't exist actually show me that I was simply a naive young woman looking for love, acceptance and worthiness outside of myself. Embracing that now is huge, because it empowers me to be the person for myself that I needed back then and to make conscious efforts to give myself the things that were lacking. And I'm sure in another ten years' time I'll be able to do the same with the experiences that I'm having now—and the same is true for you.

Let's put a stop to the notion that you have to either hit the delete button on your past or be Pollyanna Positive about all the crap or mistakes that you've endured...and simply embrace what has been as what was. Lean into the achievements, the progress, the survival...but also the messy, shameful, regretful moments and how they've combined to get you to this point right here. The point where you decide to stop letting the past dictate your present or your future, and allow it to be your springboard into the epic business and life that is available to you and awaits you.

Intuitive Insights

1. *What limiting beliefs or old stories are stopping you from taking action and moving forward? How can you start to reframe these?*
2. *Which primary fear personality is holding you back? How can you begin to take small steps to challenge this fear and kick it to the curb?*
3. *What are some more positive ways that you can respond when your Business Survival Mode is triggered?*
4. *What are your core boundaries and priorities in business/life and how can you tighten up any leaks around these?*
5. *Where are you letting unrealistic expectations mean something about you? How could you break these goals or expectations into more manageable/realistic ones?*

3

Rewrite Your Story

Not too much longer after my adrenal fatigue diagnosis and after the tone of people around me changed from 'You amaze me' to 'You need to slow down,' I had a pivotal moment (or a quarter-life crisis moment) that was a wake-up call for me.

It was part-way through 2017 and it had already been a huge year of growth in my skincare business. We had relocated into a *huge* warehouse, further expanded our distribution into the United States, began moving pallet loads of stock and launched a number of new products. For the first few months of the year, I was also still working full time in a corporate counselling role, so more than forty hours of my week were allocated elsewhere. I was juggling a lot—constantly messaging Chris on my phone during work meetings, doing Instagram posts in the toilet, co-ordinating stock and manufacturing on my lunch break, and spending my forty-five minute commute reading business blogs. It got to the point in mid April, where Chris and I decided it was finally time to leave my full-time job and focus solely on our business. I was so excited to have more than forty hours of time back that I could dedicate to growing our business, but it wasn't quite the seamless adjustment I expected.

A few weeks after leaving my job, I was struggling. I was so used to having a routine schedule of going to work for eight hours a day that I felt lost with all of my newfound time. I didn't quite know what to do with myself, and suddenly felt like I was on the clock in a new way—only this time I was responsible for the results *and* my livelihood. I felt an immense pressure to fill my day with countless tasks to show myself that I was committed and productive. It seemed that any moment I *wasn't* working, was a moment that dollar coins were dropping down the toilet. It was a big transition for me to be responsible for how much money or engagement came through the door that day—a very different experience to showing up to a job and knowing you'll get your paycheck, even if you don't achieve much.

Chris and I started getting into a groove around working and living together, and had key responsibilities, tasks and systems that we focused on so that we rarely clashed. On the outside, things were going good…really good. I was finally the entrepreneur that I knew I was destined to be. It was empowering and exciting in many ways, but it also came with new pressures and expectations that I hadn't experienced when I was working in traditional jobs. I was often feeling out of my depth, terrified of messing things up and felt like I could never let myself switch off from creating the success we wanted.

One day, I was standing in our huge warehouse, looking at pallet loads of stock along the wall ready for a big international order, seemingly 'living the dream' when I dropped to the floor and burst out crying. I felt so completely hopeless, lost and anxious. I felt like my dreams were bigger than my ability and I was constantly chasing my tail. I hadn't exercised in weeks and felt like I lived and breathed our business.

'Surely, running a successful business wasn't supposed to feel like this?!' I thought.

It wasn't, and it isn't.

But I'd let so much of my inner critic, limiting beliefs and self-doubt take control that I was completely disconnected with my power and what I needed so that I could be in a place of aligned and inspired action.

It was in that moment that I realised I needed to change my attitude towards how I showed up for myself and my business...

Up until that point, I hadn't really heard of business coaches and I wasn't listening to any podcasts or had any business supports around me, other than my partner.

But I knew that it was up to me to start addressing my needs and become the writer of my own story, so I started diving into my psychology training and accessing business supports to begin to shift the narrative.

'Your thoughts create your reality.'

It was a concept I'd heard of before but hadn't really understood until after my minor breakdown moment, and at that point I felt it in my bones.

'Of course—all of the negative and anxious thoughts I'm having about myself and my business are manifesting into my external world,' I thought. This was a whole body awakening for me because until then I'd spent a lot of my time complaining and blaming external influences for how I felt. Nothing was ever my fault and I wasn't taking responsibility for my role in my own life. And if I really was the only one to blame, then blame

myself I did, to the point of dropping into a shame cycle and meticulously calculating how I could make sure I would never repeat this mistake again (hello, OCD!).

It was time to start taking responsibility for myself and my life. It was time to take the power back and own my thoughts and actions—mistakes and all.

Was it scary? Of course! But it was also necessary to put myself in the driver's seat of my life, to become the writer of my story, and it was actually an extremely empowering moment for me to put myself in control of my life.

I was being called to separate from Ego. The part of us that generally rules our perspective of the world based on our experiences, identity, beliefs and environment.

It was time to take a look from the outside in and realise how my thoughts, emotions and actions were shaping my experiences and how I could begin to actively change how I was showing up in my internal world, so I could change how I was showing up in my external world.

I realised that there wasn't only *one* way to run a business and that I needed to consider my unique combination of personality, lived experience, skills and vision to give myself permission to do things differently—and support others to do the same.

Rewriting the Beliefs That Form the Plot of Your Story

When it comes to rewriting your story, what we're really talking about is reframing your beliefs about yourself and your life thus far, and how your perspectives and choices moving forward are entirely within your control.

Like I mentioned in the previous chapter, it's not about taking a huge eraser to the parts of your past that are uncomfortable or traumatic, it's about taking a huge step back from all that has been and embracing how it has all accumulated to this point. Maybe the past and your stories about yourself have been running your life. Maybe they've been preventing you from connecting with others, having loving relationships or going all in with your business dream. But the fact that you're here right now reading this book tells me that you're ready to show up for yourself. You're ready to shed the version of you that is no longer serving your biggest desires, and you're ready to step into the next part of your story. Because hey—your story isn't done yet and there is so much opportunity and fulfillment right around the corner for you if you choose to allow yourself to be worthy of it and open to receiving it.

The worst feeling in business or life is feeling stuck. Like you're dragging yourself through thick quicksand and going nowhere fast, standing in front of a huge brick wall that feels insurmountable, or like you're running on a hamster wheel over and over again.

But what if you weren't *actually* stuck? What if it was simply a lack of clarity in your direction? One of my coaches says that when you don't know the way, any road will do, and sometimes this can present in our lives where we do busy work, mindless work or get so caught up in our own heads simply because we haven't designed a clear road map of our desires.

While you believe that you can't move forward, don't have the answers, or are unable to achieve the life that you want, then you are perpetuating your stuckness. If you're going to be able to step into creating the impact and income that you desire in your business, then you need to believe in your ability to take the steps forward and restore your trust in achieving all that is possible for you. And that begins with reframing your thoughts and rewriting your story. Changing the narrative that you've been embodying and finally saying 'Enough!'

As you'll learn in this chapter, your external reality reflects your internal reality, so taking control of your thoughts and choosing to reprogram them is the foundation to going on and manifesting your ideal lifestyle. Success doesn't just land in the lap of people who don't have the inner stuff sorted, so this is why we start here.

Over-giving Susan vs Overflowing Sienna

Let's talk about *Over-giving Susan*. She's juggling business and life—barely, and often feeling mentally exhausted and drained. Her energy is always low, but she has no choice but to keep pushing on as she rushes across too many competing demands. Despite doing 'all the things' like posting daily on social media, perfecting her website, creating valuable content and offering her services—she's struggling to get results despite her efforts. She gives most of her time and energy to others, which makes it near impossible for her to show up as her best self and she constantly feels frumpy, neglected and overwhelmed. She finds it hard to make clear decisions in a timely manner or know where to focus in her business which often leads to procrastination, delayed results and burnout. Because of this she struggles to make a consistent income because she's unable to show up frequently for her audience or get visible in the right ways—which also creates an air of desperation around money. She wants to contribute to the family income by pursuing her passion, while also being present for her family and herself—but constantly feels torn between choosing business or life at the expense of one another.

Do you often feel like Over-giving Susan? I know I certainly did before I knew how to make business and life work together on my terms.

Now let's talk about *Overflowing Sienna*. She's calm, well-presented, aligned, organised and intentional in how she shows up. She has a clear way of managing her schedule for business and life so that there is time and energy allocated to both areas—without having to multi-task or 'choose' where to make sacrifices. She builds her business around her ideal lifestyle so she can achieve more while doing less, without compromising her results. She oozes magnetic energy that allows her to expand her reach and be seen in a bigger way by her ideal clients, without selling her soul to social media or chasing clients. She shows up fully for her business *and* her life, in a way that is present and free from guilt, overwhelm or procrastination. She is self-guided and makes trusting decisions on her path forward, choosing to share content and offers that feel truly aligned for her and her ideal clients, allowing them to see her as a no-brainer option to work with. When set-backs arise or things don't go to plan, she doesn't let this hold her back and simply redirects her attention towards resolving the issue and making a more informed decision. She overflows with energy, abundance, impact, connection and presence across all that she does.

Is this how you'd like to feel and act when it comes to showing up in your business and life? The Intuitive Impact Approach that I share in this book, is what supported me to become Overflowing Sienna. It's now time for you to step into becoming

Overflowing Sienna too, and my job is to support you to go from *Over-giving Susan* to *Overflowing Sienna*. So let's get to it...

Choose to Be Different

One of the biggest mindset shifts you can make in your entire life is recognising that you have the *choice* to change, to be different. When you stop blaming external forces for your situation and empower yourself from within to take action, you become unstoppable!

But this decision also comes with a sidekick—belief. You need to *believe* that you have the capability, motivation and strength to change and be different from how things have always been.

So how do you believe in yourself?

We're all born with this naïve confidence that we can achieve things. Babies learn to walk, talk, run, read and have many many times where they fail or fall down...but they continue to try again.

Over the years, life experiences and stories may have ground you down and made you question your ability...but if you can adopt that childlike belief in yourself that you *can* master skills and goals then it becomes easier and easier to take the action and improve.

Your belief may only start at about 20%...especially when you're new to something. But as you maintain a positive mindset and allow yourself the opportunity to try...your belief will increase as your results and confidence does.

Nobody starts out perfect at anything. Athletes, movie

stars, scientists, business owners...all start with a *choice* to be different and to try their hand at something that they're passionate about and *believe* that they have the ability to learn and grow over time.

So today, that choice and belief begins for you...

Forgiving Yourself and Others

In order to move on from the past and step into your new way of being, you may need to release what's happened previously and forgive yourself (and possibly others) for what has transpired. Maybe you look back on the past and wish you could have done things differently, or sooner, or maybe you beat yourself up for how you handled things or let fear take control of your decisions...

Whatever it is, it's time to appreciate that all of these events and experiences are what have gotten you to this point today and they no longer need to dictate how you live your life...

1. Write down a list of things that you feel are still holding you back. Things you regret, resent, wish were different, feel shame about, lead to self-doubt etc.
2. Underneath each one, write one or two positive things you've learnt from this situation or experience that you can be grateful for.
3. Say to yourself that you release your attachment to this situation, allow it to remain in the past, forgive yourself (or others) for what transpired and release it as having no

hold over your future actions.

I want to say here that I fully respect the fact that people have experienced traumatic and discriminating situations in their lives and it's not always as simple as 'focusing on the positive.' I appreciate that some experiences can't easily be forgotten, forgiven or re-framed and this kind of toxic positivity can be more harmful in some situations.

Everyone is on different journeys and relates to their experiences differently, so it is completely up to you to decide what you feel comfortable working through (perhaps with the support of a therapist or health professional where appropriate) and to leave what is not within your scope currently. And that's perfectly okay.

Overcoming Challenging Thoughts and Emotions

As I referenced in the last chapter, The Mindset Funnel is something I designed to conceptualise the relationship between our internal and external world. It illustrates the popular concept that your thoughts ultimately create your reality, and can offer a way to feel more in control of your internal world and how you present yourself externally.

THE *Mindset* FUNNEL

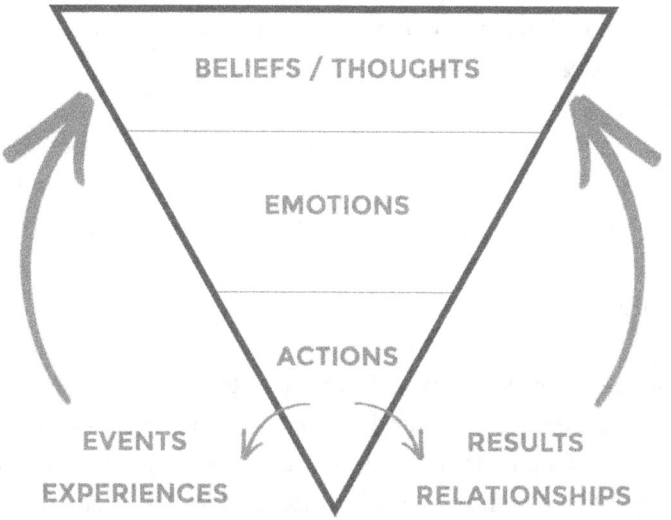

© Wellbeing Weekly

Beliefs/Thoughts - Essentially, our version of reality is made up completely of our thoughts and personal interpretation of the world. It is completely subjective. Two people may experience the exact same event, yet have completely different thoughts about it. These thoughts and beliefs then inform our emotional responses.

Emotions - Depending on the nature and context of your thoughts (positive or negative), they will elicit particular emotional responses. Sometimes these emotions are completely subconscious reactions to a triggering belief/thought.

Actions – Based on the combination of your beliefs/thoughts and associated emotional response, you will demonstrate relevant behaviours/actions that are directed by your internal experience.

Results/Outcomes – The combination of your thoughts, emotions and actions then dictate the results, outcomes, or experiences that you have in your life. You then perceive these outcomes in the form of beliefs/thoughts and the cycle continues.

Independent Outcomes – I want to note that there are some situations/outcomes that happen to us that are completely outside of our control or influence. These can be things such as freak accidents, natural disasters, traumatic childhood experiences...but our beliefs/thoughts about these experiences then commence The Mindset Funnel process.

Post Traumatic Stress vs Post Traumatic Growth

Some people respond to a traumatic event as a source of growth and use it to give back or support others, while some people respond to a traumatic event as a source of stress and prolonged suffering.

This notion forms the basis for the Warrior Energy Archetype, as this person has often endured hardship or trauma in their lifetime and have chosen to share their story as a source for helping others. They connect through sharing their experiences and build energy by knowing that they've supported others by how they have overcome their struggles.

An example of this could include two women who both lost their partners in the 9/11 terrorist attack. One woman may use this experience as fuel to begin a charity and support group to assist widows of terrorist attacks or unexpected tragedies, while the other women may spiral into depression and become unable to work which further exacerbates her depressive symptoms.

Neither of these responses are more 'correct' or 'appropriate' than the other, but it illustrates how different people who have experienced the same trauma can respond differently. You too get to choose what is the best response for you, and perhaps that involves a combination of responses that play out over time.

Intuition vs Inner Critic

A common question that comes up with my clients is 'How can you distinguish between your intuitive voice and your inner critic?' It's an important question because sometimes your intuition can warn you or give you a 'gut-feeling' about something, but this could also closely resemble irrational fear reactions.

For example, you might feel a resistance towards taking a certain action in your business and you're not sure whether it's your intuition telling you that it's not in alignment or if it's a fear of rejection/failure that it may not work out.

It's a fine line and can take some practice listening in to what your mind and body is trying to tell you before you can better distinguish whether it's coming from a place of self-service or a place of self-sabotage.

One key way that helps me to distinguish between my intuition and inner critic is the timing around when I've felt/heard/seen the message. Often intuitive 'hits' come through very quickly and randomly, before you're able to really think too deeply about the details.

Feelings like 'I need to travel to America' or 'I need to reach out to this particular person' or 'I don't want to speak at that event' that come through without knowing the how/why/what.

In comparison, the voice of your inner critic is often a more delayed response that can very commonly follow an intuitive hit. It's the feeling of doubt, fear, or embarrassment that can come after an inspiring moment or exciting idea that then makes you start to question yourself. For example, let's say you get a feeling that you don't want to send a particular email to your email list, but if you start to think things like, 'I need to email my list if I want to stay relevant' or 'people will forget who I am and never want to work with me'...then it's usually safe to say that the initial gut feeling is your intuition and the following fear based thoughts are your inner critic.

In which case, I recommend exploring your initial thought/feeling and why it is that it's coming up for you. Is there something you need to reconsider about this situation or action? Could you move forward with it in a way that feels more aligned to you?

Comparisonistis

A huge issue that comes with social media and the ability to see into others' lives so easily, is that is can be cause for comparison. 'She's doing so much better than me,' 'She looks like she has the perfect relationship and is so happy,' 'She started after me and is already making more money,' 'I'm doing all the same things but she is getting so much more attention'...and so on. Sometimes you'll be conscious of when you're comparing yourself to others and other times you might not even realise the impact that certain people are having on your confidence. If you notice that you feel sad, isolated, defeated or hopeless after seeing content from certain people, then I recommend muting their content or unfollowing them. The truth is that social media is just pictures that don't tell the full story, so as you begin to rewrite your story, it's important not to take on the highlight reels of others as your ideal. Everyone has their own issues and struggles, and over the past year we have seen seemingly 'perfect' social media couples breaking up.

Something that really helps me when I find myself comparing to others, is recognising that what I envy in them is something that I know is possible for me. If you find yourself wishing you had something that another person has, it simply means that you're conscious of your capacity and ability to achieve it too. People act like a mirror to our internal world, and you can choose whether to let the reflection get you down or inspire you to change.

Oftentimes my struggles with comparison come from knowing I could be stepping further into my potential to have the results that others have. So instead of beating myself up for being a failure or a loser, I embody the feeling of what it is that I want and affirm that it is possible for me too, then I get to work on what I need to do to make it a reality in my story!

The Writer of Your Story

The beautiful thing about seeing your life like a book that is still yet to be written is that you get to define your journey and what it means to be successful in your business and life.

Your life is yours to live.

Like we've already covered, you decide where you prioritise your time, what you value, where you spend your energy and how you decide to show up in business and life. And with that, you are the writer of your story. You are the one filling the pages each and every single day with your journey. If you don't like the way the story is unfolding, put in a plot twist!

If you thought about your life so far as a novel, how do you feel? Are you happy with how the story goes? Are you proud of how the story goes? Or are you left feeling like the best is still yet to come?

Good news. There's still time and many blank pages left to fill.

Embracing and articulating your story is not only important from a personal perspective, but also from a business perspective. As a personal brand, your story is what makes you unique and helps you to stand out from everyone else doing the same services as you. Your unique experiences, challenges, hardships, breakthroughs, triumphs and achievements all combine into a story that makes you, YOU!

Being able to share openly and vulnerably about your story within the relevance of your brand and niche can be so powerful to help you attract & connect with ideal clients—who most likely are going through what it is that you've already overcome. So many of my clients tells me that they chose to work with me because they could relate to the stories I share.

There is immense power in your story, and there are people who are searching online at 3 a.m. for stories just like yours to resonate with so that they know they're not alone in their struggles and they find hope in you.

Here are three different ways that you can use stories in your business and branding:

Signature Story – Your main brand story that covers your own similar challenges or relatable experiences to your ideal client, and the details of your own positive transformation to the point that you are now in a position to support others to achieve their specific goals. This is typically the story that you will see on people's website about page, sales pages, social media posts, or woven into free content like webinars or blogs.

Snippet Story – Snippets or segments of your main brand story that you simplify and shorten for different situations. You might have four or five key snippet stories that zoom into particular parts of your overall signature story and go a little bit deeper on a specific experience and lesson.

Sunday Story – I named it a Sunday Story because it refers to your day to day or 'everyday' stories. These are the experiences that happen to you along the journey of your life and are not key to your overall branding but are relatable to your audience and can provide a key lesson:

- Everyday mistakes, setbacks, complaints etc. Something not going to plan.
- Situations where you're demonstrating that you're 'only human' and have days where you don't always practice what you preach.
- A random experience that you can relate back to the transformation you provide people.

You're in the Control Seat

The moment that The Mindset Funnel clicked into place for me, was the moment a new world of possibility and empowerment opened up. I was no longer a victim of my circumstances with life just 'happening' to me.

I realised that I was in control of the reality that I created for myself, and I could *choose* how I showed up for myself internally and externally—you can too! Even if I made the wrong choices on certain days or made silly mistakes, I knew that I still got to wake up the next day and choose again.

Sometimes this simple change in perspective can be the most ground breaking and transformative 'aha' moment that my clients experience. It puts you in the driver's seat of your life and in control of creating your own reality—when you allow yourself.

Intuitive Insights

1. *What limiting beliefs need to shift so that you can choose to show up differently and believe in your ability to get results?*
2. *What situations/experiences do you need to let go of and forgive so you can release their hold on you and move forward positively?*
3. *How will you rewrite your story up until now and determine how it unfolds moving forward?*
4. *What challenging thoughts or emotions are currently holding you back from your goals, and how can you begin to shift these with more positive, empowering beliefs?*

4

You 2.0

'I'm going to start a podcast,' I said to my partner Chris and waited shyly for his response. We were away for a week on a holiday over the 2017 Christmas period and I'd had this burning inside me to begin sharing my voice about wellbeing and mental health in the business world. Despite this, the thought of putting myself out there was *terrifying* and I'd rehearsed the conversation of telling Chris, so I could come across as more confident about this seemingly random decision. His response? 'Go for it!'

I'd been on this journey throughout the year of showing up better for myself, addressing my needs and improving my approach to my business, and podcasts had been a huge support to me during that time.

But I felt like something was missing in podcast land...a representation of my story. All of the podcast episodes seemed to focus on the success stories, the rags to riches stories, the stories of how someone made $30,000 in two weeks with zero audience. Sure, these were inspiring...but I found myself scrolling for the 'not so shiny' topics. The conversations around the real life of running a business, support for those struggling with their mental health or mindset when growing a brand, and the fear/limiting beliefs/doubt. I *had* the money... but I was still miserable—and no one was talking about that.

And so I decided I was going to bring a voice to it.

After my first declaration, I spent about a month questioning my decision. I started thinking of all of the people that might hear me and what they would think of me. Which would then switch to thinking of the embarrassment if no one listened to me and what *I* would think of me.

I'd never owned a personal brand and I'd had the luxury of hiding behind a product business that didn't require me to show up and share myself. But the landscape online was changing and people wanted to connect with real people and I knew that if I went forward with this, the thing I was selling was myself.

I took a step forward in the only way that felt comfortable at the time, to name it something that didn't use my name and didn't require a picture of my face.

I had a range of brand names that I was tossing up between and couldn't seem to make a decision on which one to go with, so I flippantly asked the universe for a sign. One of the options was Wellbeing Weekly, and later that day I opened an email from Kikki K and the top product featured in their email was their 'Wellbeing Weekly Planner' and I decided in that moment that the sign had appeared.

And the Wellbeing Weekly Podcast was born.

Beginning a podcast and putting *my* voice out there for the world to hear was the biggest step of confidence in myself that

I'd taken. I had no fancy equipment or recording space and simply took messy action by recording my first podcast episode on my phone voice recorder. I did that for my first few episodes, before Chris bought me a proper microphone for my birthday a few weeks later. That's when I knew I was committing to this, and that it was going to take me stepping into a new version of myself to bring this brand to life.

A version of me that was confident to share my message with thousands of random people, to share photos of myself, to put my name behind my work, to share about myself publicly on social media and face judgement and fear, to step into my strengths of combining psychology and entrepreneurship to help other business owners achieve their goals.

It really was a process of stepping into Michelle 2.0, and positioning *me* as the product.

The New You

In order to achieve your goals and make your ideal business and life a reality, you need to commit to taking courageous action and thinking, feeling and acting differently...

You've probably heard people say 'fake it till you make it' and while I don't believe in being fraudulent or manipulative in how you present yourself or your business, when it comes to 'acting as if' you may find that many of the things you want in your life or the type of person you want to be, are accessible to you right now.

It firstly takes a commitment to yourself, that you are worthy and deserving of stepping into your next level. I remember for a number of years I struggled with staying consistent with exercise. I would start a new training program for a few weeks and then slowly stop doing it. I wanted to be fit and lose some of the extra kilograms I was carrying, but I realised was that part of my issue was that I didn't feel like I deserved to exercise. I felt like exercising was time taken from other things—especially my business—and I noticed that I didn't really love myself and my body enough to want to make it better. I wasn't willing to invest the time in myself as an act of self-love, because I didn't feel deserving of indulging in myself in that way. As I realised the underpinnings of flaking on workouts, I was able to work on the underlying issues and understand how important my physical fitness was to my mental health, self-image/confidence and time away from my business. It was then I was able to shift my perspective and commit to showing up to my fitness in a more empowered way.

One of the most important precursors to actually working out who it is that you *want* to be, is acknowledging that the change is possible for you. Many people are stuck in a fixed mindset where they believe who they are now, is who they'll always be. That there's no opportunity for them to become *more*. This is where people limit themselves to predestined life of living within limits and not allowing themselves to grow. It comes from the same mentality as those who say 'people never change.'

As a trained psychologist, my whole career was based around the belief that people could change. Why would health professionals exist and people seek help if they couldn't change? We are *all* capable of change. You get to decide in any given moment if something no longer serves you, if something (or someone) in your life is not aligned, if you're participating in behaviours that are not conducive to your wellbeing or the wellbeing of others. And you get to decide what takes its place.

There may be many evolutions of you throughout your lifetime and that is perfectly okay. As we grow and learn, we evolve our thinking and what's important to us. As our lives change or have new things/people added to it, we may change what it is that we value and where we want to spend our time. Deciding that there's a new you on the horizon doesn't mean you're forever fixed as that person. It means that at this moment, you're being called to upgrade and step into more for yourself, and you may do that many times again. That's the beauty of growth and making the decision that things are going to be different for you.

So if you don't first believe you can change, then that is your work for now. Shifting into a growth mindset where the possibilities to become what you desire are within your reach— even if it's one small step at a time.

Once you feel the call for more and believe you are worthy and capable of embodying it over time, then you're ready to receive it...

Who Do You Need to Be?

How do you need to think, feel, and act differently in order to become this new, empowered version of yourself?

How would someone who has what you want to have be thinking, feeling and acting?

What aspects of this can you start to bring into your life now?

For example:

1. If a person with your ideal business and life would make time to learn and better themselves then how can you commit to that now and implement that with this book?
2. If they would invest in their own wellbeing and self-care, how can you begin to add more of this into your life?
3. If they would get up each day and dress well and do their hair, how can you ensure that you add this into your morning?

Write a list of all the characteristics, habits, beliefs and actions that the next level version of you would have and do, then see which ones you can begin to embody as of today.

Who You Were, Isn't Who You Are

One of the issues of being stuck in the past, is believing that who you used to be, the things that happened to you or the things that you did will dictate the rest of your life.

This is simply not true. Every day we have the chance to change and rewrite how our story unfolds. Who you were, isn't who you are or who you'll always be—it's up to you!

The past serves as a guide for us to be better now and into our future. The past is nothing but a memory...so imagine—how would you think, feel and act if you had no memory of your past?

The phrase 'living in the past' means that you're letting things control you that are long gone and giving your power away to your 'old self' or other people. Use your past to lift you up rather than bring you down.

How amazing is it to think that 'who you are' and your future can still be largely unwritten? As I always say, you never know what tomorrow will bring!

Shine Your Light

I love the idea of shining your light. I think it's such a beautiful way to explain how you share your gifts with the world and make someone's day or life a little brighter—just for being you.

There's a lot of darkness in the world, and you may even find that there are shadows within yourself that you struggle with. That's okay. We all have our shadow side that we need to work through and acknowledge, but that doesn't mean that the light in you has to be dimmed.

When you shine your light, you illuminate others with your gifts and create a ripple effect that can support them to also shine their light. Whatever it is that you do to help people in the world, that makes a contribution to bettering their life and situation so they can continue shining in their brilliance. It becomes like a fairy light display of people glowing with their gifts and serving one another around the world.

When you dim your light, or worse—don't believe that you have a light to shine—the world is a little darker and less blessed by your gifts. Someone out there who needs you, doesn't get to cross your path or doesn't get to experience you in all of your radiating glory.

Everyone that you reach with your light becomes changed

and illuminated in a new way. All work is impactful. All work makes an impact on people's lives in one way or another. Where would we be without garbage disposal, plumbers, hotel staff, bus drivers? While some people's work might not impact your life too much, it doesn't mean that they don't have a monumental impact on the lives of others. The same goes for you, there may be people who aren't impacted by your work because it's not for them, but there are others who will be so damn grateful that you chose to shine your light their way.

So harness your light, believe in your light, and as you follow the call for a more intuitive impact—shine your light.

Your Permission Slip

Sometimes I see situations where women feel that they need someone else's blessing or approval to align with their dreams and follow their heart.

I know I've felt this myself. It was largely due to a lack of trust in myself and a fear of taking responsibility of the outcomes. I'd always ask everyone else 'What I should do?' or 'What do you think of this?' or 'Should I do this?' That way I could trust my decision more, or shift the blame if something went wrong.

This was a form of co-dependency on others and was anything but empowering. I realised I needed to *stop* going outward and *start* going inward. Knowing that I had all the answers and resources inside of myself, and that I knew how to find them for myself if I wasn't sure of something.

The more you go inward and call on yourself, the more you

will trust yourself, the more confident you will feel in your decisions and the more likely you will be to take action towards your goals.

So, here's your permission to write your own permission slip...

You don't need confirmation, advice, opinions or input from others if it ends up holding you back, questioning yourself, or leaving you dependent on others to achieve your goals. You've totally got this!

You Won't Be Seen by Everyone

As you're embracing the new confident and empowered version of yourself that is ready to show up and be seen, there can be an expectation that you'll start to be seen by many people. But if you're staying true to your genius zone and carving out an aligned niche for yourself, there will be many people who don't see you. They might watch your content or come across your social media posts, but they won't really *see* you. It won't be enough to trigger them to want to be part of your world or work with you.

This has nothing to do with your capability or influence, it simply means that they're not ready for what you offer or they're not in need of what you offer, and that's okay. It can be easy to feel defeated and rejected when it appears like people aren't recognising you for your efforts. I've been there before and it can feel like there's something wrong with you—*'Why don't people care what I have to say?!'* But when I switched my perspective to sharing value for the pure joy of it and letting go of the need for particular results, that's when the results actually appeared. If you struggle with constantly creating content and feeling like you're chasing clients, then I suggest trying to switch your perspective in this way and focusing on sharing value from your heart...trusting that the people who need to see it will see it.

When you show up in that way and stay true to your vision, your niche and what you can offer people, you allow yourself to be truly seen by those who need you. This is how you attract clients who like, know and trust you because they also feel seen by you.

It's ok not to be seen. It doesn't mean you need to discount yourself, dim your light or change yourself or your offers. Not everyone will like you, and that often means more about them and their own judgements than anything to do with you. There will be people who don't need what you offer and choose someone else, or there will be people who may not need you until six to twelve months in the future.

When you show up as you (the You 2.0 that you're stepping into) you will be seen by the people who need to see you, at the time that is right for them to see you. Allow yourself to be seen.

Follow the Call for More

As we move into Part 2 of this book—Embrace The Present—it's time to heed the call for more. Letting go of the limiting beliefs as they appear, pushing through fear, forgiving your past self, going inward and giving yourself permission to follow your own dreams.

If you're anything like me, you've been called to this work via a fire in your belly and burning passion in your heart to help others and have a bigger impact and income than what you've currently been achieving...

Just like in the hero's journey (or basically any popular movie plot), the hero (that's you) has to acknowledge and hear the call to take action. Some people can feel this but let fear, doubt and insecurity hold them back from ever truly acknowledging it. Don't be that person. The inner calling and purpose won't fizzle until you choose to follow it.

So let's follow it together...

Intuitive Insights

1. *What do you need to add, remove or change in your day to day to step into the new version of you and who you want to be?*
2. *What would you say to your future self in five years if you continued to let the past hold you back and hadn't moved forward on your goals?*
3. *Why do you feel that you need external permission? What's driving that? In what ways can you begin to go inward with decisions before going outward?*
4. *What are you being called to do? What is the passion and purpose bubbling within you and how can you commit to follow that calling?*

II

Part 2 - Embrace the Present

5

Create Space for More

'But I don't believe in God...,' I thought to myself as I kept hearing about the importance of spiritual wellbeing and tapping into your source energy.

It all sounded a little woo woo to me, especially coming from a background of over six years of psychology training and experience.

But as I was continuing on this journey of diving deeper into myself, listening to my intuition, and confidently building personal brand, I started to realise that spirituality could mean anything I wanted it to—and didn't need to be connected to religion.

I knew that my spiritual wellbeing was lacking. I'd been so focused on my mental, emotional and social wellbeing lately that I hadn't really considered how I could integrate a spiritual practice into my life.

The first step I made into the arena of spirituality, was

deciding who my chosen 'source' was. I didn't associate with a religion and I sometimes struggled with the concept of fate or the universe having my back. I wanted to keep my power as my own and not place it externally to me, so I decided that my source of belief/power/knowing was myself. Just an ideal 'better' version of myself—my higher self.

So I began an evening practice before I fell asleep of tuning into my higher self. How would I act if I wasn't afraid or anxious? What would I do in my day? How would I show up online? What would I share? How could I take one step closer to becoming my higher self?

I also started focusing on a regular meditation practice and ended up completing a Meditation Teacher Training so I could share my own meditation recordings with the world. At the time of writing this book, one of my morning meditations has over 80,000 plays!

To take my meditation and 'zen time' further, I joined my local yoga studio and attended three to four classes a week. Initially, I would find myself tearing up in most classes as I was getting better and better at slowing down and tuning in. It was such a cathartic process of switching off from my day and allowing myself to stop and listen to what I needed in the moment. I had so many intuitive hits and messages pop in during yoga classes and I finally realised how important a consistent connection to my spiritual wellbeing was for my personal and business growth.

I'd spent my whole life running. Running forward, running from thing to thing, and running away. Creating space for mediation, yoga and connecting to my inner world forced me to stop the running and open up to what was there in the spaces in between.

That my worth and 'enoughness' wasn't measured by how many businesses I owned, how much money I made, or how many tasks I could cram into my to-do list. It was all there, inside me...even when I was laying on a yoga mat doing absolutely nothing.

I finally started to learn how to slow down, find joy in the journey of life, and embrace the present...

There's No Time Like the Present

One of the key things I learnt from one of my early mentors, author Eckhart Tolle, is that there's no time like the present.

In fact, there is no other time than the present...

The only actual moment that we can capture is the present moment. What's behind us is a memory and what's in front of us is a desire.

This might leave you feeling like you need to seize every moment and never relax, but I actually want you to consider that life is made up of billions of these tiny moments, so we have time to create the space for what we want to spend our time on.

In each moment you can choose how you want to spend your time. Some moments will go by without anything interesting happening, some will go by with difficult things happening and some will go by with great things happening.

But the more you can begin to tune into your present moment, rather than being stuck in the past or caught up in the future, the more you'll be able to make decisions from a place of presence and create space for what you want to call in.

So how do you tune into the present?

It can be as simple as just noticing. Noticing what's going on for you moment to moment, being aware of your environment, seeing or hearing the things you normally wouldn't notice. Things like the air-conditioner or birds outside, being conscious of what you need in this very moment and honouring that. This is also known as a mindfulness practice.

Relax Your Body, Calm Your Mind

You've probably heard of mindfulness and meditation by now, and possibly practiced it a little (or a lot) yourself.

Mindfulness and mediation practices are a fantastic way to relax your body and calm your mind. To bring your awareness out of the depths of thought and into the present moment where you can detach and then reconnect with yourself.

There are a number of different ways to practice mindfulness or meditation and it really depends on what resonates most with you, fits into your lifestyle and gives you the desired results of calm and inner being.

It's also important to note that mindfulness and meditation doesn't need to mean that you sit on a cushion in a robe for one hour in complete silence.

There are ways to integrate these practices into your everyday lifestyle, and can be done in as little as five minutes!

It also doesn't mean that your mind will be completely free of thought or *blank*. While it can help to divert your attention from difficult thoughts or challenging emotions, our brains are designed to think.

So mindfulness and meditation serves to support us to better 'sit with' these thoughts and emotions, and to let them process and pass by with less impact over time.

Mindfulness Activities:

- Exercise mindfulness (walking, running etc, and tuning into surroundings)
- Eating mindfulness (being conscious of taste, texture etc, as you eat)
- Senses (picking a sense and tuning into how that feels in the moment—sound, smell, taste, touch, sight)
- Activities like 'find something in your environment starting with each letter of the alphabet' or 'pick colours and then find something around you with that colour.'
- Spending five minutes in silence just noticing how you feel and what you experience in the present moment.

Meditation Activities:

- Body Scan Meditation – guides you through a process of relaxing your entire body.
- Guided Meditation – talks you through a process of relaxing your body and calming your mind. Can be themed like anxiety, loving kindness, gratitude.
- Visualisation Meditation – guides you through visualising a particular journey such as grounding in a forest, walking along a beach, connecting with a loved one.
- Music Meditation – chimes, bells, singing bowls, nature sounds etc, that you listen to as you meditate.

- Silent Meditation – period of silence often distinguished with bells where you have no guidance or background music as you meditate.

You can listen to my popular morning mediation audio by searching for 'Michelle Kerr' on the free Insight Timer App or clicking here...

The Gift of Gratitude

Something that has had a huge impact on how I view my life, and how many others do too, is having a gratitude practice.

Gratitude simply means connecting in to what you are thankful for—what is already part of your life, part of your personality, part of your being that you can appreciate and give thanks for.

The more that we can connect with what we *do* have (however small or big that may be), the more we can create space to bring MORE into our lives.

If you're not grateful for the things that you already have (potentially things you take for granted that others dream of having), then how can you expect more to come into your life when you're not accepting of everything you currently have?

I have two simple gratitude practices that I run through before falling asleep each night and it might be something that you can integrate into your routine too.

1. Three Gratefuls
2. Never Ending Gratefuls

Three Gratefuls

1. Something good that happened today that I'm grateful for.
2. Something bad that happened today that I'm grateful for having the lesson.
3. Something that hasn't happened yet that I'm grateful for the opportunity to manifest.

Never Ending Gratefuls

Basically run through all the things you're grateful for that you wouldn't normally notice much and keep going until you drift off to sleep (kind of like counting sheep!).

For example—I'm grateful for the roof over my head, I'm grateful to be in a warm bed, I'm grateful to have pajamas, I'm grateful for my belly full of food, I'm grateful that I got to work on my passion today, I'm grateful for speaking to my mum on the phone and so on.

Delete, Delegate, Digitise

Now that we've covered some of the more internal shifts for freeing up space in your life, let's dive into some of the more external ways to create more space. One of the productivity tools that I share in my coaching programs is Delete, Delegate, Digitise.

As the name suggests, this is all about looking at the tasks and responsibilities that you've taken on in your business and life and determining whether you can apply one of the three D's to it.

Delete – This one is pretty simple. It's no longer serving you and time to delete it from your schedule and your brain space. You'll no doubt find that when you actually track all of the minute tasks that you do in a week, there will be many things that don't need to be there. Maybe you've committed to helping your mother-in-law with something that is draining you or you're promoting a number of offers that aren't actually selling or feel good. Maybe you're committing to things that aren't getting results rather than focusing your efforts on what is working. Maybe you're shaming yourself into doing things around the house that just Don't.Need.To.Be.Done. Whatever it is, it's time to hit the delete button and free yourself.

Delegate - Identifying tasks or responsibilities that can be shared with another person (partner, family member, child, team member etc.) or that you can hire someone to take care of. Examples of this might include hiring a podcast editor, a cleaner, a virtual assistant, asking your partner to take on more household tasks, or asking your mother to pick up the kids from school and take them to swimming on Wednesdays. Many of my clients (and women in general) are taking on far too much of the mental load in their lives out of guilt, expectation or the desire to feel needed. Let's shift the narrative, drop the guilt, and delegate the tasks that are overwhelming you or preventing you from working within your genius zone.

Digitise - How many tasks in your business or life are you taking on that have the potential to be automated or digitised? It's amazing what technology can do these days, but often so many women I speak to are still doing things the long, labourous way.

A perfect example of where I've digitised in my life this year, is ordering all of my weekly groceries online. It saves my previous list and I simply add it all to the cart with any quick modifications or additions and it's all ready and waiting for me to pick up the next day. Not only does this save me the time of walking around the supermarket racking my brain on what to buy, but it saves me huge *mental* energy because I don't have to think. Winner. Maybe there's things you can digitise in your business or life—automatic email chains, scheduled social media posts, robo vacuums, online form submissions rather than sales calls, automated payments from your bank, purchasing templates for your work assets and more!

Just by tracking all that you do in any given week, will allow you to review your schedule with a critical eye and determine where you can add *hours* into your week. Which means more time doing the things you love and being with the ones you love.

The Power Of Batching and Repurposing

Another productivity tool that I shout from the rooftops is both batching and repurposing. Running a skincare company, you better believe I learnt all about batching early on and how to get the maximum output (stock) from the minimum input (time). An example that I love to use is baking muffins. Usually you'll get yourself a recipe or a muffin mix that allows you to bake twelve to twenty- muffins in a thirty-minute period. But what if I asked you to make each of the twenty-four muffins from scratch individually? You would need to mix up 1/24th of the recipe and then pop it in the oven and repeat the process again for the next muffin. How long would that take you? *HOURS.*

Similarly, if I was to ask our manufacturers to make up the formula for one bottle of skincare at a time, rather than a larger batch that makes five-hundred bottles at once—their time and our time would be severely wasted.

So the same is true when it comes to batching business and life tasks. How can you combine similar things and batch them into one big recipe of a task. For example, if you have a podcast or a blog you could set aside a few hours a month to produce four pieces of weekly content that is ready to go, rather than sitting down each week and going through the whole process individually. You could batch similar errands so you can get them all done in one car trip, rather than having to go out numerous times across numerous days. You can buy your weekly groceries in one big batch, rather than grabbing bits and pieces every couple of days. You could have a set hour for email replies, rather than letting it distract you from your tasks throughout the day.

There are so many ways to batch things in your schedule to free up not only more physical time, but also more mental space for yourself.

The next phase of that is repurposing. Think back to the muffin example. Instead of baking six muffins for school snacks, you might bake twenty-four muffins and have school snacks, something to take to the family lunch, some for the freezer for emergencies, and maybe even some for yourself!

Repurposing in your business is often most crucial when it comes to content creation. There's a hundred platforms and places we're 'supposed' to be showing up but that doesn't mean you have to reinvent the wheel every time. When you create a core piece of content for your business, let's say a blog or podcast episode, you can then repurpose that content by sharing excerpts and adaptations of it on other platforms. Consider what your core piece of content could be each week, and how you can take that one piece of content and repurpose it across all of your other business assets. *Simples!*

The Spaces in Between

Have you ever caught yourself in a moment of doing nothing? If the answer is no, then this chapter is one you'll want to come back to. I like to call these moments the spaces in between. Where you're in between tasks, or responsibilities, or find yourself in a moment of stillness. So often people will fill these spaces with something immediately, because being in stillness is hard. It can feel lazy, or unproductive to give yourself a moment where you don't have anywhere to be or anything to do.

But there is so much power that comes in these spaces, when you can embrace them for what they are. Peaceful, tranquil moments in time where you separate from your ego and you can just be. These moments can be confronting and uncomfortable for anyone who has made it their mission to always be doing *something.*

But just like the Hustler Energy Archetype, it can soon become apparent that these efforts to always be busy and productive are avoidance tactics for sitting with who you are, and through burnout you can become suddenly forced to sit with yourself in the quiet and evaluate what got you there.

So how can you embrace these moments more in your everyday life, so that sickness or burnout doesn't land you there? You allow them, and relish in them. You might even choose to create them with some of the techniques mentioned earlier in this chapter. But the next time you find yourself in between with a moment to spare, allow it. Allow yourself to sit on the couch and take a breath, allow yourself a moment to stop and look at the sky, allow yourself a cup of tea without any other distractions, allow some wind down time before you fall asleep.

These moments are pure presence. Where you're not fixated on the past or anxious about the future...you just *are.* When you think about it, this moment is all you have. It's the only moment that is real and tangible, it's the only moment that you exist in. The more you can capture yourself in the present moment and detach from the responsibilities and the ego, the more space you create for intuition to enter.

The Journey (Not the Destination)

When you're creating space for more, whether it's the opportunity to rest, practice self-care, or the opportunity to reach your goals...you can use presence as part of that goal setting.

It's so easy to get caught up in the destination. 'When I have X,' 'If X happens then I'll...,' 'I won't stop until I reach X.'

What happens with this focus on the end goal, is you forget to notice all of the amazing action taking, lessons and growth that happen on the *way* to that goal—the journey.

You may be missing out on all the little wins, the overcoming of fear, the changes to your priorities, or the willingness to honour your needs that all happen in the present moment of going after your goals.

So how can you remind yourself to bring your focus back to the journey?

- Journaling regularly about your progress
- Celebrating your small wins—sharing in groups, posting on social media, celebrating with friends/family.
- Gratitude practice.
- Meditation and mindfulness to tune into where you are in your journey.
- Allowing space, rest, and self-care to make your journey more sustainable.

Intuitive Insights

1. *What are you creating space for in your life? Where is there space for 'doing' and where is there space for 'being'?*
2. *What mindfulness or meditation practices align with you? What could you commit to adding into your current routine to allow you to tune into the present moment?*
3. *What does expressing gratitude look like to you? How can you regularly show your appreciation for all that is already yours?*
4. *In what ways can you celebrate the journey of reaching your business or life goals?*

6

Love Thyself

'You always get it done,' a phrase I'd frequently heard from people. Prior to my quarter-life crisis moment I was a self-confessed 'do-er'. Unfortunately, this was often at the expense of my own wellbeing.

I'd frequently pile up my to-do list with as many things as possible, stay up late, work weekends, skip friends' events or family catch ups to keep working. I'd got myself to a point where I'd neglected exercise, hobbies, and connections in pursuit of my goals.

We're served the message as entrepreneurs and business owners that you need to 'hustle until you make it,' 'never give up' and 'don't stop until you get results.'

I was fully plugged into this mentality and I felt like any time I wasn't working was time that took me further away from my goals or meant that I was a lazy entrepreneur with no drive.

The issue with this mentality is that it comes from a very

'masculine energy' and fails to acknowledge many of the other areas of our lives that help us to be successful. Also as a woman, it often neglects the fact that we're usually also growing or caring for children and devalues the importance and time commitment of that responsibility in our lives.

As I spent more time at my yoga studio and was becoming more and more confident showing up online, I started to become better at acknowledging my need for self-care and time away from working.

I realised that the success of my businesses was reliant on how 'well' I was and that a big part of me being in my optimal energy, motivation, and purpose was to ensure I was filling my cup and taking a holistic approach to my wellbeing. If I was going to preach and teach the importance of wellbeing in business to others, then I was determined to integrate it in my own life first.

That's when I started to learn more about 'feminine energy' and how vital it was for me to have a balance of both masculine and feminine energies in my businesses and life.

When I'm in my masculine energy, I'm working on the outside stuff. I feel like nothing can stop me—I'm motivated, tick off tasks promptly and productively, show up confidently on social media, pump out content and get results. I'm taking action and moving forward in a way that is visible to others.

When I'm in my feminine energy, I'm working on the inside stuff. I'm introspective, creating from a place of flow, taking breaks or practicing self-care, cuddling with my dog Koda, journalling and planning my next moves. I'm taking action and moving forward in a way that is only visible to me.

These energies don't have to operate independently of each other. I've found a way to integrate them both into my day where I can have moments of solid action taking followed by a cup of tea in the sun. But by acknowledging the importance of looking after myself first and foremost, I've detached from the identity of always having to be *doing* rather than *being*, and I've significantly improved my ability to give from a place of overflow to others in my life and business.

Because if you're not functioning well, how can your business?

But First, Love Yourself

Have you ever heard someone say that in order for others to love you, you first have to love yourself?

Whether you believe this or not, we can use this notion within your business. If you don't love yourself, your business and your offers...how can you expect others to?

I know that it's not as simple as deciding one day to 'love yourself'. Especially if you're grappling with self doubt, failed expectations or traumatic events/experiences that have impacted how you see yourself.

But that doesn't mean that you can't ever love yourself. You most certainly can. Like everything in your life, it's a choice to start working on loving yourself.

Before you can truly love yourself, flaws and all, you need to first move through self-acceptance. Like anyone or anything that you eventually love, you will generally begin with accepting them as they are and for what they add to your life. The same is true for you.

Beginning to accept yourself, even if you're not where you

want to be in your life, is the starting point to loving yourself and treating yourself well.

How would you feel about yourself if you could accept yourself like you do a small child? You might laugh off their mistakes, love them unconditionally, understand that they're learning and growing...

So how can you give yourself the same grace?

One of the biggest things that has helped me with self-acceptance is separating myself from my flaws/mistakes. Believing that I am not my mistakes, I am not my past and there is more to me than my insecurities.

It takes time and conscious practice to bring yourself back to a space of acceptance, respect and love for yourself—perhaps even if others don't feel the same. But when you can tap into this regardless of what anyone else thinks, you become so powerful.

Treat it like an experiment, like you're forming a new relationship only it's with yourself. Go easy on yourself, have fun with it and begin to acknowledge what makes you lovable or what you'd like to work on to grow your self-acceptance and self-love.

You Are Not Selfish

How many times do you think *'I'd love to do X, but...?'* But I have no time, but the kids need me, but I'm saving money, but I have more important things to do, but I should be working. One of the biggest issues that women come up against when it comes to doing things that involve fun, self-care, self-indulgence or rest is that they feel selfish and guilty. Like their time is not their time anymore, especially after having children, and that all of the other priorities of life need to come long before they prioritise themselves. Society depicts the mother who sacrifices time with her children for time on her own needs as not being a 'present' or 'attentive' mother. It depicts business owners who sacrifice time working on their business for time on their own needs as 'lazy' or 'undisciplined.'

I'm here to tell you clearly: self-care is not selfish. You've probably heard this or seen it in cute social media quote pictures, but it's an imperative perspective to hold if you want to ensure that your energy needs and wellbeing are addressed. When you give, give, give, and nothing is given back to you— it's a fast route to resentment and burnout town. We need to normalise spending time, money, and energy on what it is that we need to restore and rejuvenate our own life force. The more that you normalise it and don't feel it needs to be justified, the more others around you will also see the importance of you having these moments.

Self-care gets to mean anything you want it to. For some, it could be that expensive massage but for others it could be having a shower in peace. When it comes to adding things into your day or week that recharge you, I always suggest to go with whatever feels good in the moment. Consider yourself like a battery. You need to manage the input of energy to recharge the battery and have it working at its optimal. If you always use the battery's energy and never replace it, eventually it will go flat and stop working—just like you. If you've ever experienced periods of burnout, overwhelm or found yourself crying on the floor of your kitchen (it's happened to the best of us) then you know the impacts of not recharging your energy and having your own sense of play and pleasure.

The people around you—your children, your partner, your family, your clients, your audience, your community—are best supported by you when you support yourself. The only person perpetuating your thoughts of guilt and selfishness are you. There are so many ways to fill your cup without it taking too much time or money away from others. It could be playing an upbeat song in the car during the school drop off, it could be spending the first thirty minutes of your work day with a clear calendar and cup of tea, it could be sitting at a cafe to write your blog instead of your desk, it could be using room spray or candles to shift your environment, it could be phoning your mum while you're walking the dog.

When you shift your perspective on what it means to recharge yourself so that you can integrate these moments into your day, everyone benefits.

Energy Vampires

As I talk about things that drain your energy, you may find that you have quite a few energy vampires around you. Energy vampires are people who basically suck the life out of you and often leave you feeling overwhelmed, exhausted, resentful or self-conscious after you've been around them. You may have a few people that come to mind straight away, or you may need to think about some of the ways that people around you are actually draining you more than they're lifting you up.

It's important to note that when it comes to identifying energy vampires in your life, that you don't see yourself as a victim of other's energy dynamics. There are many ways that you can protect your energy from people who may drain you and to be able to maintain positive relationships with them moving forward. It's also important not to identify yourself as someone who can 'be drained.' This often means that you find yourself in a constant state of defence and protection, when really you have the power to shield your energy from being drained in the first place. By feeling like you're someone who always needs protecting or has sensitive energy, you can find yourself attracting the very people that you need to protect yourself from rather than empowering yourself to attract those with a higher vibration.

As an introvert, my energy can be easily drained by other people but I've had to be conscious of not having that become part of my identity. Even people with good intentions or who I enjoy having in my life can be draining for me if I'm around them for long periods or have murky boundaries with my time. There have been many times in my personal and professional life where I've allowed myself to spend too much time with people and been left feeling drained and unable to give myself to other tasks/responsibilities that day. These people are in no way rude or difficult, but I only have so much energy to give to others and I need to be mindful of how I schedule time with people. This is another reason why I only schedule client appointments on particular days and in particular time blocks, so that I'm able to manage my energy needs and ensure that I'm able to support my clients from a place of abundance rather than depletion.

You may find that there are people in your life who really do suck the life out of you. Rude, inconsiderate, self-absorbed, disrespectful people who don't deserve the energy that you give to them. If you notice that when you're around certain people you find yourself feeling less than ideal, then this is usually a sign that something needs to shift in the relationship and how you're allowing this person to treat you. Or it may be time to throw some garlic at that vampire and rid them from your life altogether.

These people may be partners, family members, friends or even clients. Just because someone has been in our life for a long time or is paying us for something, doesn't mean we need to keep them in our lives forevermore. You get to choose who you surround yourself with and how you protect your precious energy, and sometimes enforcing new boundaries or letting someone go are the best things you can do to be aligned with the ideal reality you're creating.

You may also find that many of the people who impact your energy are well meaning and are simply projecting their own limitations onto you as a way to protect you. Common example of this are friends, family members or partners who may insist that you get a more secure job or let go of your business dreams because they are not instantly successful. Often these people care about you greatly and are trying to help you avoid failure, criticism or financial loss—but many of these things are part of being a business owner and taking risks to make your dreams a reality. It's hard not to listen to these people and it can often mean that your light is dimmed, but if you can appreciate that only you can see your vision and bring it into reality then it can become easier to let the comments of others be water off a duck's back.

Put Yourself Back on the To-Do List

A big part of demonstrating self-love—or even at a minimum, respecting your needs—is to make sure that you're doing things that light you up and feel aligned with bringing you joy.

So many women that I speak to neglect their own wellbeing or needs at the expense of others, but over time this actually means you're less able to support others adequately, because you become burnt out or resentful.

Demonstrating self-love and self-care can come in a range of different forms, and it's ultimately up to you to recognise what you need most and to demonstrate that.

Here are some ideas for adding more self-care and self-love into your life:

- Rituals (shower after work, cup of tea before work)
- Routines (set activities throughout the day that recharge your energy)
- Hobbies (sports, crafts, reading, writing, gardening etc.)
- Community Groups (mums groups, business groups, running groups etc.)
- Self Soothing (inner child work, trauma work, item of clothing, environment etc.)
- Self Talk (affirmations, journaling, meditation)
- Practicing what you preach and living your message—solidifying what you believe

Seasons and Cycles

I write more about supportive cycles for business and productivity in a later chapter, but I think it's important to touch on the cyclical nature of life as it relates to how we treat ourselves.

Life moves in seasons and cycles. It's why we have night and day, winter and summer, moon cycles and menstrual cycles. One of the laws of the universe even refers to this with the Law of Cycles, indicating that everything rises and falls, waxes and wanes, increases and decreases. In the earlier days of our ancestors, this law was understood and appreciated. They knew that there would be times of feast and famine, that there would be times of stark cold and sizzling heat, that things would be going well only to be followed by more difficult times. As technology and civilisation has advanced we've come to look at our lives as being more linear than cyclical. We expect everything to improve over time in a linear way...our knowledge, our income, our assets, our family. And while we know that nature moves through its cycles, many forget to embrace the cyclical nature of life.

There may be times in your life where you're not doing well in your business followed by times where you are doing well. There might be times where your life is full of growth and abundance, and times where it is full of loss. There might be times where it feels like everything is going just how you wanted it to, followed by times where it feels like everything is falling apart.

Life isn't linear. It moves in cycles and seasons, but the one thing that remains constant is that there is always change afoot. That a bad, hard, or cold season doesn't have to mean that the next season is the same. When you can embrace that life moves in cycles and realise that the good can balance with the bad, you can become more resilient in the process of living and survival. You're better able to hold on for the storms to pass, or appreciate that if things suddenly turn sour it doesn't have to unbuckle you. You begin to understand that business can move in ebbs and flows, especially when it's your own business, and be able to foresee and navigate these waves.

It's the same with your relationship with yourself (and even others), where there may be times where you've struggled with self-love or self-belief coupled with times where you've backed yourself and gone after what it is that you want. Just because there are moments of pain or failure, it doesn't mean that becomes your story. These moments are inevitable in life *for everyone* and are seasons that we move through and move to birth new ventures and situations in the next season.

Follow Your Own Path

Cultivating self-acceptance, love and respect is a personal task that can only be completed by you. If you don't have these in place for yourself, you may notice that your external reality mirrors this with people being rude, abusive or pushing through your boundaries.

It's important to build your confidence and 'armour shield' so you can follow your own path. Following your own path is especially important when it comes to your business. If you allow competitors or the success of others impact how you feel about yourself and your ideas/potential, then you're putting your power in other people's hands and letting them dictate how you move forward with your passion.

Put the Blinders On

As a business owner, it's often essential that you put the blinders on and stop absorbing content or updates from anyone who makes you feel 'less than.'

Here are some ways you can reduce your 'comparisonitis' and focus on your own path:

- Unfollow, mute or block anyone who makes you question yourself or feel inadequate.
- Create content separate to social media so you're consuming less.
- Stop absorbing or signing up for content from competitors.
- Reduce how much you listen/watch things that bring you low vibes—news, blogs, podcasts.
- Celebrate your small wins.
- Connect with people at a similar space to you so you can support each other.
- Remember that you never know someone's full story and social media is often a highlights reel or what people 'want you to believe.'

Be Your Own Biggest Cheerleader

Something I learnt early on in my first business is that I need to be my own cheerleader. Friends and family don't always understand what you're doing, and people can place their own insecurities on you (ever heard 'You should get a "real" job?!').

At the end of the day, if you can't back yourself and be confident in what you're doing then you can't expect others to. Believe that you're your own biggest fan...because only you can see the vision in your mind and know the feeling of alignment and joy.

Even if things don't go to plan, when you support yourself to try then you never know what opportunities, new ideas or pivots could emerge. If I didn't forge on with my skincare business, I wouldn't be here writing this book for you today!

Go Inward, Not Outward

Maybe you've had those moments of intuition or a gut feeling of what you want to do in a particular situation, but you've doubted yourself and gone with the advice of someone else—only to regret it.

I want to encourage you to flex your self-trust muscle and practice going inward before you go outward. Ask yourself things like 'What would I like to do in this situation?' 'What would I do right now if I had no one to ask/help?' 'If everything worked out in the end, what would I do right now?'

When you're the face of your business, trusting yourself becomes even more important because it becomes a reflection of your brand. If you're mimicking what other people are doing, showing up in a way that feels inauthentic, or creating offers out of a need for money rather than passion...it can often mean the results don't happen in the same way for you.

Always trust in your ability, your ideas and what feels right to you at your core. Where you can be yourself and not be afraid to share what matters to you. Because that is what resonates with YOUR audience and the people who need YOU. I've always found that when I take action based on trusting my intuition, it builds my confidence to take that next bigger leap of trust until I feel more and more confident in taking my own directive.

Intuitive Insights

1. *What would your life look like if you accepted and loved yourself as you are? What would it feel like? What would need to change to get to that place?*
2. *What acts of self-love and self-care can you add into your day or week so that you prioritise your needs and have a spot on the to-do list?*
3. *What needs to change to support you to stay focused on your path and not succumb to comparison?*
4. *What would things look like if you were your own biggest cheerleader and trusted yourself first and foremost? How can you make this a reality?*

7

What Do YOU Want?!

'What do you think?'

'What should I do?'

'Can you just check this for me?'

For most of my life I trusted other people's opinions over my own. As a self-confessed perfectionist, battler of OCD thoughts and always trying to prove my 'enoughness'—there was no room for mistakes. So it became standard for me to ask everyone else around me (including Google) to weigh in on my ideas/decisions/goals and validate that I was on the right track. This all came from a good place of not wanting to make mistakes or accidently hurt anyone, but the issue with this behaviour was that the only person who could know if I was on track, was me.

I gave my power away so much, because it provided a protection and an excuse for me to blame others when things didn't go to plan. 'But you said xyz,' 'But everyone thought it was a good decision,' 'I wouldn't have done it if you didn't say it was okay' and so on. It was a way for me to spread the blame so that if anything went wrong or my ego was bruised, I didn't have to fully absorb the pain of admitting that it was my decision in the first place.

After I started being aware of this habit and how much I was giving my power away to others to tell me the answers (often thanks to a very self-aware partner who would politely ask me to decide for myself), I worked hard to overcome this habit and claim back my power.

I called this going inward, before going outward. And oftentimes when faced with a big decision or goal, I would ask myself what I thought the way forward was and not ask anyone else's opinion. It was tough as first, but as I started to trust more and more in my decisions and take responsibility for the outcomes, my confidence grew.

As my podcast and personal brand was growing, and I had started offering coaching services, I began to notice that I was giving away my power in new ways. I was no longer reaching out to friends and family for advice, but I was turning to others in the coaching space to tell me what I needed to do to have a successful personal brand. How to market online, how to grow an audience, how to find new clients and so on...

I began losing trust in my own business knowledge and found myself in constant states of confusion if I didn't have a coach or mentor around me. I was looking for someone to tell me the answers, rather than finding them inside myself.

I got roped into the online world of service provision and passive income—the promises, the manipulative tactics, the selling strategies, the urgency, the fabricated credibility...

And I ended up selling a coaching program that wasn't fully

aligned with my strengths. I believed that I needed to sell what people would pay for, over what I wanted to provide, and then made myself believe that it was what I was passionate about.

Don't get me wrong, I built a fantastic online program and supported many wonderful clients in their businesses, but I knew deep down what I *wanted* to provide and what I *was* providing were not one and the same.

My original aim with the Wellbeing Weekly brand was to combine my psychology and business experience to bring a voice to the challenges that can come with growing your own business, and to shine a light on the mental and emotional impacts of entrepreneurship. Like dealing with the expectations to succeed, the anxiety around getting results, the pressure to generate an income, and the isolation as you build your brand from the ground up.

As 2020 passed by, and I worked with more and more clients about strategies, marketing tips and email funnels—I felt that I was also moving further and further away from my original aim and what it was that I wanted to be known for within the brand. I was out of alignment with my genius zone of supporting women to move through their perceived limitations and step more powerfully into their ideal business and life.

I remember thinking that my business name reflected why I had started the business, but not what I was currently offering and I found myself trying to bend the meaning of the name to justify it in my head. I knew deep down I was veering off track and was going to need to make a decision (on my own) about how to get back on my path.

A big revelation and lesson for me last year, was to hold tight to my original vision, get clear again on what I wanted moving forward, and to not let myself be steered in other directions or lose sight of that.

What Do You (Really) Want?

A big part of staying true to yourself, is being clear on what it is that *you* want in your business and life. Not what other people want, not what your clients want, what YOU want.

You can have all the clients in the world, but if you're doing work that doesn't light you up or keeps you in your bliss zone... then it's going to slowly eat away at you.

When you're looking at embracing the present, it's helpful to have clarity on what it is that you actually want. What is it that you're striving for right now? What do you wish life could look like?

Sometimes people don't even take the time to clarify what it is that they want. They think they 'know' what they want, such as to be rich or have a big house or financial freedom. But these are vague goals that don't encourage change.

You need to know what it is that you really want. What does it mean to be *rich*, what does it look like? One person might consider rich being $100,000 a year, while another might need $1,000,000, while another might see rich as being able to spend time with their family without worrying about money.

Determining the details of what you want or how you want things to look for you, is what will help you to get there. You might even realise that you're already on your way, or even have some of the things you thought you wanted!

Having clarity on the details will also help you to take action on these things NOW and stop them from being some far off goal or wish. For example, if you want to buy a house, what can you be doing right now to support that? Looking at the market, improving your credit, saving for a deposit etc.

You're Already There

Now that you've spent some time getting clear on what you *really* want, I want to let you in on a little secret...

You're already there!

Everything that you need to make your goals a reality, is already inside of you. Who you are—your personality, your drive, your passion, your creativity, your belief—already exists inside you right now.

You've just got to keep tapping into it and allowing yourself to grow with every small step you take. For every far off future dream or goal, you've already got the ability to make it happen today, if you choose to not give up and keep going.

It's already written, if you believe it to be so.

What Lights You Up

You may have worked out by this stage of your life, that doing things you don't enjoy or that drain your soul—are no fun.

But, it's also true that you can't spend your time doing things that light you up *all* the time...or can you?

There's things that come with being a responsible adult like dishes, doing taxes and changing nappies...but that doesn't mean you need to get stuck only doing things that bring you no joy.

Sometimes it can be a matter of perspective change. Complaining about having to look after the kids vs thinking that you GET to spend time with your kids.

Sometimes it can be a matter of prioritising the things that bring you joy and making time for them in your life...allowing yourself to laugh, to create, to love, to play.

I have a saying that I say to myself most nights before I fall asleep:

Help me to move towards the things that light me up and to move away from things that no longer serve me.

I may not always know what isn't serving me or what I should be doing instead, but I put it out there that I'm willing to observe and take action when it does become apparent to me. It might not happen instantly, and I might have to do things I don't love doing for a while—but I'm constantly moving closer to what lights me up.

Your Bliss Zone

Something that I conceptualised in the early days of coaching was 'The B Box.' This is a tool to identify tasks or areas of your life and which category they fall into based on how they make you feel: Blah, Bored, Busy and Blissful. It's also then derived further based on what you desire and what you're good at.

The goal of The B Box, is to segment your everyday tasks and responsibilities in business and life so that you can clearly see which tasks fall into your bliss zone and which tasks can either be deleted, delegated or digitised because they're just not your jam.

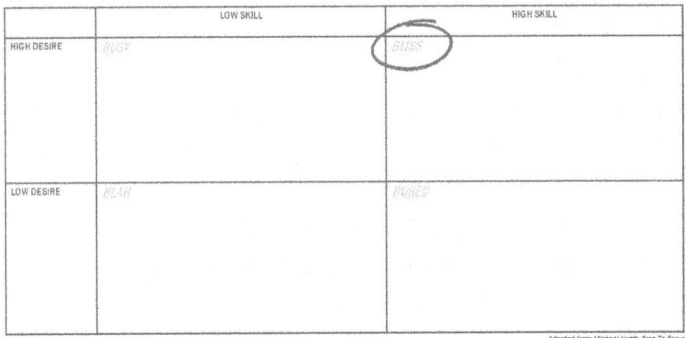

Adapted from Michael Hyatt, Free To Focus

Ideally, the tasks that you have a high desire to do and that you're highly skilled in will fall into your bliss zone. For me these tasks include things like creating podcast episodes, coaching clients, running my group program, writing and speaking about my passion topics and spending time with my family.

You'll often find that tasks where you have a high desire but low skill become your 'busy' work, where you procrastinate or get lost doing so that you don't have to do other things. An example of this could be tinkering on your website because you enjoy being creative, but you're not all that skilled in optimising websites. Your 'bored' tasks are those that you're really good at but have no fulfillment or enjoyment from doing. These could be things like creating social media graphics or editing videos/podcasts, and are often best outsourced to those who are highly passionate about that area (where it's *their* bliss zone). Then finally, the 'blah' tasks aren't something you enjoy doing or something you're good at—hence feeling blah about them. These could be things like cleaning the house, reaching out for collaboration opportunities, accounting tasks or anything that just doesn't float your boat, and are best delegated or deleted where possible.

If you find that at this phase of your life that you're unable to remove or redirect any of the tasks in your B-Box and need to continue to do them, then it's imperative that you're making time for the things that fall into your bliss zone. Often the things we enjoy doing can be the first to fall off the schedule to the less important but more urgent menial tasks.

Coming Home to Yourself

Just like Dorothy from *The Wizard of Oz* would say: There's no place like home.

The fastest way to shift into full alignment is to step into your authenticity and truth, and let go of being who you 'think' people want. When you can show up in your full quirky, honest, vulnerable brilliance, you not only connect more fully with yourself but you also allow others to connect with the true you.

So many people go through life feeling like they're living someone else's life or are 'so deep' into their dynamics that it's too hard to change things—don't be that person.

It's time to come home to yourself...

Our external reality often acts like a mirror, and we can

use this to go within and realise what we need to resolve, accept or improve. If you want to feel safe, secure, loved, believed, trusted, heard—you need to first feel all of these within yourself.

If you can feel safe in yourself, love yourself, believe yourself, trust yourself, listen to yourself, then you open up to allow others to do the same. Other people can't be your belief, or your trust, or your security—this all needs to start within yourself and that's when you can begin to feel more at home within yourself.

How do you come home to yourself?

Inner Child Work: Our inner child is the version of us that may be wounded or traumatised from our upbringing. It can be the part of us that feels unloved, unworthy, unheard, and unacceptable, so to start healing these parts of ourselves we can begin to 'mother' ourselves. You might consider what you would say or do to your child (real or imagined) if they we're feeling this way, and then offer this to yourself. Perhaps it's a big hug, perhaps it's reminding yourself that you're safe now, perhaps it's noticing all the evidence of where you are loved/wanted/accepted etc.

The Answers Are Within

Going inward rather than going outward is how you can build trust, belief and confidence within yourself. When you constantly go outward for answers and base your actions on other people's feedback or thoughts, you give your power away and can move further out of alignment.

Have you ever had a moment when you follow someone else's advice and say to yourself, *'I knew I should have done what felt right to me?'* That's your intuition speaking, and more than often you know yourself and your business better than anyone else. You know what you're trying to represent and your big vision that others can't quite grasp.

So do you, go within and believe that you constantly have the answers inside of you.

Don't Overpromise

Something that I see all too often in my clients is impostor syndrome. This refers to the feeling that you're not good enough or worthy enough of the income or impact that you're gaining. That you feel like a fraud and are afraid of being *found out*. This feeling is so common that even superstar actors, singers and athletes experience moments of impostor syndrome and question how it is that people see value in their skills.

Where I see impostor syndrome playing out for my clients (and when I've felt it myself), is overpromising in their services or offerings. By overpromising, I mean that they create services or offers that support people with things that they're not quite confident or skilled in delivering, because they think it's what they need to offer. They get lost trying to prove themselves as being able to provide everything but the kitchen sink, so that clients choose them. It ends up backfiring because they don't have the confidence to promote themselves properly or feel out of alignment and never mention the service.

I always tell my clients that it is best to create services within the bounds of your skills and confidence. You can stand out as being an expert in a niche space that you're passionate about and confident in, rather than feeling like you need to offer results that are outside your current scope. I see this as a strength, and a leaning into your specific genius zone rather than an indication that you don't know enough.

For example, a plumber might have superior skills in solving pipes impacted by tree roots and have a particular interest in preserving trees whilst also supporting households to have adequate plumbing. However, instead of leaning into being an expert in root damage he feels that he needs to promote all kinds of plumbing services on his website, that he's not all that confident in. This leaves him feeling the effects of impostor syndrome when he is hired and paid to do alternative jobs that he doesn't feel completely skilled in. If he were to lean into root damage and promoting his values around the importance of this area of plumbing, he would be far more likely to promote himself, build referrals, and even position himself as the leading person in this niche.

The other side of the coin when it comes to letting go of impostor syndrome and working within your bounds, is to qualify yourself. And by that I don't mean go and get more degrees (unless you *really* need to), but to determine your own worth and value based on what you already know. You get to decide how you feel about your skills and experience, and how qualified you feel. Another degree or certificate or training isn't going to fill the void if you don't believe that you're worthy and capable. There are people out there doing exactly what you want to be doing right now, with less skills and knowledge than you. So sometimes it becomes more about making the decision that you *are* qualified to do the work you're doing, and start doing it.

What Does Success Mean?

When it comes to thinking about what you want in your business, most people say something along the lines of success, wealth and freedom. But have you ever stopped to think about what those things actually look like to you? Success, wealth, and freedom can have very different meanings and manifestations for every single person. What I consider to be a sign of success in my business, may be completely irrelevant for you. The same is true for wealth and freedom. Freedom to me could be spending the majority of the day at home with my children while making money in the background, where for you it could mean staying at a beach house for two months of the year.

Because of these nuances, it's important that you define what success means to you. Write a list of all of the things that you will have, be or do when you consider yourself to be 'successful.' This will not only help you to be clearer on how to bring these desires into your life, but they'll also help you to know when you've achieved signs of success. You may even realise that you've already achieved some of the things that are important to you.

It's also important to make note of what you've been letting success mean up until now. Perhaps you've subconsciously been afraid of success because of the not so shiny things you've been letting it mean. These could include things like success means that I will out-earn my friends and they won't want to spend time with me, success means that I won't be able to spend as much time with my family, success means that I will out-earn my husband and bruise his ego, success means that I will be seen as greedy or self-indulgent. There are so many money and success stories that you may be holding on to that you're not even aware of, so this can be a powerful exercise to release these blocks.

When I did this myself, I realised that I had been letting success mean poor mental health. I was concerned that with success would come more work, more responsibility and therefore more overwhelm and pressure, causing me to feel unable to cope. This was subconsciously preventing me from going after the very things I wanted, in order to maintain my wellbeing. I needed to reframe this belief and realise that impacting more people with my work and being compensated for my passion/purpose actually meant *optimal* mental health and *more* time with the people I love. This simple reframe meant I was able to step more confidently into attracting the success that I want.

Intuitive Insights

1. *What is that you really want in business and life? Be specific. Keeping vague goals provides an excuse not to reach them.*

2. *What truly lights you up and brings you joy? What doesn't? How can you move further away from what no longer serves you and closer to what lights you up?*
3. *What does your inner child believe that is no longer true and needs to be healed and nurtured? How can you mother yourself?*
4. *What needs to shift internally or externally for you to be able to turn to yourself more for the answers you seek?*
5. *What does success mean to you? What would it look, feel, be like to have 'success?' What have you been letting success mean up until now that may be holding you back?*

8

Step Into Your Power

'There's no baby, this pregnancy isn't viable...'

In that moment, on a bed in the ultrasound clinic at eight weeks pregnant, time stopped and my world collapsed. It was the last thing I expected to hear heading into my first ultrasound, excited to hear my baby's heartbeat.

I didn't know what to say. I didn't know what to feel. I was numb. I remember fighting back tears and trying to appear strong, but inside it felt like every part of me was crumbling.

We left the clinic empty handed, got in the car, and I burst out crying.

I was having a miscarriage. I'd always known it was possible, but I never thought it would happen to me. All of a sudden the baby book I'd been writing, the baby blanket I'd been crocheting, the baby announcements I'd been planning were all void. No one even knew I was pregnant yet, and now I wouldn't have the chance to tell anyone.

After a crazy year of lockdowns and pandemic hysteria throughout 2020, we were so excited to end the year on a positive note and celebrate that we were having a baby. Even better, my due date was on my thirty-second birthday. I felt like everything had fallen into place, until it all fell back out of place and into a jumbled mess of emotions, grief and what-ifs.

Following that appointment, I drove to my mum's house and burst out crying in her arms. She didn't even know I was pregnant and now I was telling her that I wasn't. I felt like all of the sparkle and excitement of having a baby was ripped away from me, and instead I only had sad news to share where nobody knew what to say. I'd been given the gift of becoming a mother and then it was taken from me, so what was I now? I felt like I didn't belong to anywhere and like the universe was laughing at me for thinking having a child could be so easy.

We moved through the awful process of miscarriage and set our sights on recovery, healing, and optimism moving forward. I decided to only tell a few close friends about what had happened, and we decided not to tell our families because we wanted to keep the excitement that comes with announcing a viable pregnancy.

At the time of writing this, our families (other than my mum) still don't know what I've been going through over the past eight months. It's something I want to share more about, because I know the darkness and pain that women often go through alone...but it needed to be the right time for me.

I needed to move through the experience and process it in my own way, before sharing it publicly. But I knew that it was something I needed to share in this book. I couldn't talk about tuning into your intuition, stepping into your aligned vision and believing fully in yourself, without talking about my miscarriage.

As you'll see over the next few chapters, it was what cracked me open and allowed me to go even deeper into myself and be able to do this kind of work more intensely with myself and with you.

For a number of months I was unsure of my purpose. While I was pregnant, it felt like my entire purpose was to become a mother and to provide for my baby. But as quickly as it came, it was taken away. I struggled to revert back to 'pre-pregnancy life' and refocus on all of the business projects in front of me. None of it felt like it mattered anymore. There were days that just ticked by and I wasn't present for myself or others. I struggled to be engaged in a life that no longer included the prospect of our baby, but I had to find a way to re-calibrate and find the path to moving forward.

At the point of writing this a number of months later, I can now say I'm grateful for experiencing our loss. It showed me a strength I didn't know was in me, challenged me to surrender, built a deeper purpose within me that burned bright, and began a bigger calling to fully step into my power and become the woman I knew was within me...

I began to find power in the powerlessness and knew that one day, this difficult part of my story would become an important part of my uprising and journey to becoming the woman and mother I desired to be.

Empowered Women, Empower Women

You might have seen Instagram posts saying, 'Empowered Women, Empower Women.'

I love this phrase because I think it really highlights how when we empower ourselves and step into our own power, we not only inspire others to do the same but we create a new culture where women are given the space and platforms to rise up into their brilliance.

It also means that we bring each other up, rather than tear others down.

Repeat After Me

Something that has become an important part of showing up more powerfully for myself and stepping into my power is repeating affirmations. Affirmations aren't for everyone, but they can be a fantastic tool for reprograming negative or limiting thoughts. Whenever I feel fear or doubt rising in me, I speak through or journal out some affirmations to switch my energy and realign with my vision.

In order to step into your power and claim your worth, you need to trust in who you already know you are. But sometimes you may need a loving reminder, and that's when affirmations can be helpful.

The most important thing with affirmations or mantras is to use ones that feel aligned for you. There's no point saying things that feel like they don't relate to you or aren't within your current realm of embodiment. You can always add affirmations or mantras along the way as you enhance your belief system.

The best way to work with affirmations is to repeat them out loud and fully feel into the energy it evokes in you. You can also write them out in your journal, or have them on post-it notes near your desk as a loving reminder of who you are and what you're creating.

Here are some of my favourite affirmations/mantras currently, so feel free to take any or all that stand out to you:

- I am worthy of love, wealth and acceptance.
- Everyday I am planting the seeds to create my biggest desires.
- I attract a bigger impact and income just by being me.
- I focus on the what and the why of my life, not the how.
- Everything is working in my favour.
- Everyday I show up as the powerful, wealthy version of myself.
- Money flows effortlessly to me in ways I can't foresee.
- Every day I move closer to my biggest desires.

Powerful Routines and Habits

What would your day look like if you were showing up as the most confident, empowered and fulfilled version of yourself? If you had the money, the clients, the family, the house, the outfits? It's very likely that it would be different to how you're showing up for yourself today. But what if I told you that it didn't have to be? That you could begin to embody the very things that the future you would be doing?

I encourage you to take a moment to write out what your day would look like and how you would be spending your time, energy and money. You may notice that there a things on that list that you can be working on right now. The thing is, your external reality can only mirror your internal reality, so if you're not showing up for yourself or making efforts in the areas that you one day hope will be a given, then it's not just going to fall into your lap. Let me tell you from experience, even when the money comes, if you don't value yourself or prioritise the things that are important to you then more money won't make much difference. You'll just be rich and miserable.

Creating powerful routines and habits for yourself starts now, *before* all that you desire is a reality. You're setting up the foundation for your behaviours to attract more of what you're already doing. Sure, it might not look exactly like the future version of you...but just because you can't sip champagne on a yacht in the Greek Islands right now, doesn't mean you can't create moments of fun, play and luxury in your life in other ways.

So in order to embody the person and business that you're stepping into, I suggest crafting some rituals, routines or habits that evoke the feelings and experiences that you hope to have as part of your every day.

One way that I've done this is by creating a dream day meditation at the suggestion of one of my coaches. I have simply recorded myself on my phone speaking out what my ideal day looks like—right now. Not in six months, or one year or five years. But right now. That way when I listen to it back daily, I focus on bringing that version of my day into reality as much as I possibly can. For the phase of my life that I'm in now, that includes things like slow mornings with meditation and journalling, working less than five hours a day, attracting clients while I'm not even at my phone or computer, having space for exercise and creative hobbies, and ample time to reflect and recharge for the day ahead. And this is exactly what I'm manifesting in my day-to-day. As my life circumstances change, so will my dream day and I'll record a new meditation when I feel that I've outgrown the current one.

So what does your dream day look like, and how can you commit to making those things available to yourself right now?

Less Doing, More Being

Something I never knew about when I started my first business was feminine energy and how to use it within my business to create more serenity and flow amongst the *work.*

I thought business owners had to hustle and grind, work late nights and weekends, and sacrifice the things in life that they wanted in pursuit of success. But that mentality lead me to feel unfulfilled in my business because it was taking so much from me, and I ended up feeling burnt out because I was doing nothing to recharge my energy or connect to my feminine power.

Resting, nurturing, reflecting, loving, trusting, surrendering, flowing...all of these come from embracing your feminine energy. But unfortunately so many women, especially business owners, tend to neglect this side of themselves because we're not taught about how we can use it to our advantage to stand firmer in our power.

Women are so powerful. We're not always given the credit we deserve for all that we do as individuals and a collective.

But we hold so much power within us. We create life—could there be anything more powerful than that? Children aside, when we harness our feminine attributes, honour our ability to contribute to a better world, and rise up as goddesses who choose to do business *our* way...we are unstoppable.

How do you get more in touch with your feminine energy?

- Diffuse essential oils, candles or incense around your home/office.
- Use room sprays, perfumes, rollers etc, to create aromatic environments.
- Meditate, journal or practice mindfulness to go inward.
- Allow for rest, rejuvenation and reflection—baths, massages, reading, laying on the couch, sleeping etc.
- Sensual or sexual touch.
- Nurturing yourself or others—cuddles with your pet/kids, doing something for you.
- Things that connect you with your confidence and femininity—dressing in a way that empowers you, doing your hair, dancing etc.

Crafting Your Brand Around Your Energy

Back in chapter one we explored my five Business Energy Archetypes and the key characteristics and energy needs that are common to each type. If you haven't yet taken my free quiz to identify your archetype, then I suggest taking a moment to complete it now at the back of this book in Chapter 13.

As you make moves to show up more powerfully for yourself and your business, a core area that I work with my clients on is their energy management and crafting their business to align with their energy needs. Here I'll share an overview of how each energy archetype thrives in business by honouring their strengths and energy needs so they can shine in a bigger way.

The Hustler - I usually say that all my clients start off as the Hustler energy type. Society conditions us this way when it comes to starting and running your own business, and we all adopt the work hard and don't give up attitude. It can also be a common result in my quiz because people want to choose the answer that shows dedication and passion for their business, even though another answer may be more suited. What I commonly find with those who identify as the Hustler is

1) They are actually frequently burning themselves out, feeling overwhelmed in their business, or like they're putting out more than they get back and are actually one of the other energy types when they step back and give themselves permission to see it.

2) They do thrive off the Hustler energy and prioritising their work, however they often need support to be able to also prioritise other areas of their life to avoid burnout or resentment—such as self-care, fun, feminine energy and a more aligned schedule.

In saying that, those who do align with the Hustler energy do their best work in longer and focused stints. They prefer to have a full day or number of hours to work solely on their business where they can immerse themselves in their tasks and make fast progress. Hustler's don't enjoy going slow and when they have ideas or inspiration come to them, they'll often sacrifice other areas of their life to bring their ideas to life. This can mean late nights, working weekends, little time off, or avoiding social engagements to work.

Their drive and commitment is admirable, and they will often produce quality results in short timeframes. Hustlers benefit from scheduling specific days or timeslots to focus solely on their business without interruption. They need clear, specific goals to work towards and thrive off seeing tangible results for their efforts such as sales, followers or reviews.

Hustlers can look to schedule blocks of more intense work periods, such as a two week launch, a business staycation, or having monthly targets—because they will usually get everything done based on their bursts of energy. They can then schedule periods of downtime where they rest and recharge. Alternatively, Hustlers can add pockets of self-care and fun throughout their work day so it doesn't pull them away from their goals for long periods. This could include a lunch break at a cafe with a friend, coming home to have a nice bath to sign off the work day, committing to no computer after 7 p.m. or other small habits or rituals to create more balance.

The Rebel - As a core part of the Rebel's personality and drive is to be individual and create their own rules, as they don't do well with being told what to do. As a Rebel, you often prefer to work in solitude and aren't quick to collaborate or outsource tasks. This means you can maintain creative control over the vibe and energy of your business, but it can also lead you to become easily exhausted by having your hands in many pots.

Rebels often avoid engaging coaches, mentors or absorbing copious amounts of business content because they prefer to follow their own path to success rather than mimic the advice of others. They have fierce confidence in their ideas and their individuality and this allows them to be seen as a breath of fresh air and to shine in business.

As this energy type you benefit from running your business *your* way. This might mean working from a cafe, sitting on the couch with your laptop, joining a coworking space, or a mix of whatever feels good in the moment. You need to share your views and special sauce with your audience in order to feel seen and valued. When you hide what makes you unique, it means that people can't truly connect with you and there is an invisible barrier to them wanting to become a client.

You thrive off being able to get results from following your own instincts and positioning yourself as anything other than another cookie cutter service provider in your niche.

The Intuitive - One of the most common energy archetypes (and probably why you were drawn to this book). Similarly to the Rebel, Intuitives thrive off leaning into their own inner world to make decisions about the direction of the business. Intuitives obviously have a powerful connection to their inner world and intuition and frequently use this as a beacon when choosing what to do next.

As an Intuitive, you benefit from doing the things that *feel good* in the moment and while this may not follow a traditional path, it gets you results when your energy is aligned with what you're taking on. Your day can be very ad hoc and unplanned, which allows you to feel into what you most want to focus on for the day. You benefit from slow mornings with a rejuvenating morning routine where possible, or incorporating plently of self-care and introspective time into your day. You may take meditation breaks, moments out in the sun, connect with others, or journal breaks throughout the day to continuously tap into your energy levels and intuitive messages.

You do your best work when you're able to connect with the energy of others and support them with their concerns. Intuitives are skilled at picking up on the energy of others and make fabulous guides or coaches because of their ability to see the unseen and tap into their own intuitive interpretations of a person's situation.

You don't do well with strict schedules or long blocks of work, so your work days should have a sense of flexibility and fun infused into them so you can flow with feminine energy and intuitive guidance on the work that is calling you in the moment.

The Creative - Another common archetype, where you thrive off using your creative ideas and works of art as a source of impact and income. You have a natural flare for beautiful things and bringing your creative ideas into tangible services or products—whether it's art, web design, online programs, podcasting or creative thought leadership.

You benefit from spending the majority of your work efforts in creative mode, such as updating your website, designing content, creating video value, or sharing your insights with your audience or clients. When you get stuck in non-creative tasks like accounting or answering emails, it drains you and may be worth outsourcing tasks that don't require your creative energy.

You thrive off a more fluid workday that leans into what you feel like creating in the moment. You're not often one to pre-prepare or batch content as you prefer to share what comes naturally to you in the moment. It's important to have creative outlets scheduled each day so that you can recharge your energy and connect with your gifts. If that's not possible from a work perspective, then having creative personal outlets such as painting or crocheting can support you to recharge outside of work.

You feel most seen when people recognise you and value you for your creations, so when you focus purely on sharing from your heart and expressing yourself through your art, clients will magnetize towards you and want to pay you for your gifts without you having to force yourself on people or convince them of your value.

The Warrior - This is the most unique energy type and not many fall under this category, but every energy type can take inspiration from the Warrior when it comes to sharing their story publicly. The Warrior has a story that needs to be shared with the world. Their story acts as a source of inspiration and hope to others who have experienced struggle and finding their strength to change their own reality. Well known Warriors can include people like Turia Pitt (severe burns survivor) or Oprah (childhood abuse victim and extreme poverty), who have gone on to share their story and inspire strength in others.

The Warrior's main objective in business is to share their story—the big story and the smaller everyday stories of overcoming. Many Warriors don't actually start a business intentionally, but rather show up and share their truth and naturally amass a following. If you have a story to tell that you've been hiding, the first step is to simply show up and share your journey.

Warriors don't often run their business in the traditional way because often times any products/services that they offer stem from them first creating a successful personal brand. They often fall into business by providing their audience with what is being asked for, whether it's merchandise, a book, online services/programs or hosting workshops/seminars.

The key is showing up authentically as yourself and serving as a source of hope and inspiration for others. Your people will naturally gravitate to you and will tell you what they want from you, which will then drive your offers and revenue.

Building your inner capacity and aligning your business with your unique energy needs, story and gifts is a big part of what I support my clients with in my private and group coaching programs. You can get in touch with me via email or social media to get more information on how I can support you to expand your capacity and build a life with more impact, purpose and intention.

Jump Before You're Ready

So how do you empower yourself to step into your power?

We've talked previously about believing and trusting in yourself and your ability, but that can only get you so far. The other 50% comes from taking *action*!

When it comes to taking action many women find themselves up against fear, doubt, excuses and time restraints that mean they continue to stay in 'planning' mode where it is safe, dreamy and the status quo isn't affected. But, you're never going to achieve the things you want in your life if you let these things hold you back and never take action towards anything.

This is why you need to embrace the concept of jumping before you're ready.

None of us are truly ready to take action on things that mean a lot to us or maybe even scare us, and if you do feel ready, then maybe you've waited too long! Just like someone about to sky dive or ski down a mountain, there's always that tinge of apprehension and risk, but they say f*ck it and do it anyway!

There's risk in everything we do in life, but would you rather look back knowing you stayed safe and 'risk free,' or that you gave it a go and can live to tell the tale?!

- Commit to one small action that you can take each day towards your goals.
- Set yourself a goal for the week or the month and focus your attention just on achieving that.
- Identify what you're afraid of or the 'worst that can happen,' then write out what you would do if those things *actually* happened (you'll normally find you can cope with them just fine, or they're unlikely to happen).
- Find a business buddy that is at a similar phase to you and you can cheer each other on or hold each other accountable.
- Find some empowering quotes or affirmations, like 'you'll never know unless you try.'

The Courage To Leap

A big part of stepping into your power is having the courage to leap/jump before you're ready, but that comes with the balance of emotions like courage and vulnerability.

You might think that these two words contradict each other, but really we can't show up and be vulnerable without demonstrating courage, and we can't be courageous without acknowledging the vulnerability of our fears/insecurities.

Remember: Courage is not the absence of fear, but feeling the fear and doing it anyway.

When I started my podcast, I made my word of the year—COURAGE. Because up until then, I had played small and let my fears hold me back from really putting myself out there. I always had one foot in and one foot out, afraid of messing up or looking silly.

So throughout that year, whenever I felt nervous or was keeping myself small I would remind myself of the word courage and would commit to taking action despite the fear. That year my business grew significantly and I launched my first paid program with a wonderful group of clients, grew my podcast by thousands of downloads and featured on other people's platforms as a guest expert.

So how can you remind yourself that moving forward on your goals will feel vulnerable, but it will also be courageous?

Maybe it's having a word of the year like me, or making a promise to someone to keep you accountable, or going all in on your business. Whatever it is, it has to feel right for you and have that fine balance of taking inspired and aligned action while processing the emotions that come with it.

One Step at a Time

On the other side of jumping before you're ready is taking one step at a time.

I like to use the skiing analogy here. You've decided to ride down the mountain (yikes!) but in order to do so, you need to take that first push and then one step followed by another followed by another. Until eventually you gain enough momentum and confidence to glide down that mountain with more speed and grace.

No one says that when you take that first leap or make that decision to do something excitedly scary that you have to make it all happen instantly. Things take time, but the commitment to trying is where it begins.

From there, it's one foot after the other, small step by small step, little win by little win, that all combines into a magnificent snowball effect that grows your business over time. But without those first steps, there's no movement and no momentum.

Intuitive Insights

1. *What does stepping into your power look like for you? What can you do to help you jump before you're ready?*
2. *How are you embracing your feminine energy? What could you add to your day or week to tap into your feminine energy*

more?

3. *What do the words courage and vulnerability mean to you? What would it look like to embrace both of these as you move forward with your goals?*
4. *Success doesn't happen overnight. How can you commit to taking small steps/actions each day or week towards your goals? How will you hold yourself accountable?*

III

Part 3 - Manifest the Future

9

Call It In

'I'm so used to getting what I want. I choose goals, and I work hard until I make them happen. But I can't control this, it's out of my hands and that's terrifying,' I said to my mum on a phone call, opening up about how I was *really d*oing. I wasn't doing all that well.

It had been a few months since my miscarriage and I'd thrown myself into work, and coming into the Christmas season things were busy with a capital B.

During my recovery process (which was amidst one of the harshest COVID-19 lockdowns in the world), I'd also had a craft-box business idea drop in that was so perfectly aligned to my personality and passions that I knew I just had to pursue it. In the midst of loss and grief around losing a pregnancy, and being isolated in our homes for over 100 days straight, I knew that this was a business I needed to 'give birth' to. It was part of my healing, and allowed me to find focus and purpose outside of losing my first opportunity to become a mother. It was a huge success which I've been so happy and proud of, but it meant juggling another business on top of what I was already managing. I started noticing that I was starting to slip into filling the void in my heart with more and more distractions.

As three months passed and I wasn't pregnant again, I was becoming impatient, irritated and concerned. I was doing absolutely *everything* I could, why wasn't it happening? I was becoming absorbed and obsessive about becoming a mother—it was the one thing I wanted, and couldn't seem to have. Everything online said that people are more likely to get pregnant quickly after a miscarriage, so I was filled with hope that wasn't being fulfilled.

All the while, I continued to show up in my businesses and for other people—sticking to my commitments, getting my tasks done and putting on a brave face. No one was any the wiser about what I was going through.

But behind the scenes, I was becoming a version of myself that I never thought I would be, and I was starting to lose myself in a far off future dream that had no timeline. I cried about pregnancy announcements, I avoided friends with babies, I scoured forums and baby websites for hours, I begged my body to do the one thing it was supposed to be able to do.

As January ticked by, I took extra care to take time away from work and spent many of my days napping, watching television, daydreaming and doing creative projects. The well-meaning people who knew about my conception journey kept saying to me 'Just relax and it will happen' (eyeroll), so I thought that January would mean I was in with a good chance. I hadn't relaxed so much in years. Nope—negative again.

After that, I realised as I was talking to my mum, that this was something I couldn't force. Even though I felt relaxed and stress free on the outside, there was an internal pressure and force around seeing two pink lines on a pregnancy test. I began to realise that I needed to call it into my life, and that required letting go, not fighting harder. All I had been doing for four months was forcing, pushing, tracking, checking, wishing. My phone photo gallery was full of pregnancy tests at numerous angles and contrasts, trying to work out if that was my month. I finally realised that this journey was a spiritual lesson for me that I could also take into business...

It was a lesson that things don't just magically appear because I want them to happen.

It was a lesson to fall into pure surrender and flow, where there are no timelines or ticking clocks.

It was a lesson to believe and trust in myself fully, that I was worthy of receiving the things I wanted.

It was also a lesson of where I wasn't aligned in other areas of my life.

As I entered February, a new month and a new cycle...I felt a shift. I knew that this month was going to be different, in all aspects of my life—whether I got pregnant or not.

I knew that I was finally going to take action to shift more into alignment with the kind of work I wanted to do in this business.

I knew that I was going to focus on my strengths and passions by writing this book and stepping into shining my light in a bigger way.

I knew that I was shedding the desperate energy of past months and feeling ready to integrate my lessons.

I knew that I was going to let go of things that were no longer serving me and make better boundaries about how I was spending and recharging my energy.

I knew that I was ready to show up as the woman and mother that I wanted to be.

I was ready to call in and manifest the business and life results that were inside my head, and create more to look forward to in my life than motherhood. My acupunturist recommended that I choose an enjoyable project that I could focus my energy into, so that day I made the decision that I would spend the next three months writing this book—not just to support all of you, but to also support me. It was time to call in the higher version of myself, knowing that all of the desires I wanted would follow when I showed up as her.

Deep Belief

We've covered conquering the past and embracing the present, and now we turn to manifesting the future and calling it into being. One of the biggest starting points with manifestation and creating the things that you want in life is belief.

If you don't believe it is possible for you, then how can you go about obtaining it or expect it to just be handed to you?

If you don't believe in yourself or your goals, that's where you need to start.

We need to have deep belief in ourselves and what we envision for our future, but then couple that with fast detachment, meaning we put it out into the universe but we then allow it to unfold however it does and not make the unfolding mean anything about us and our capabilities.

It's easy to make things mean something about you, but often they have nothing to do with who you are as a person. You're worthy of your goals regardless, so when you can believe in your innate worthiness you can also begin to receive all that you are already worthy of.

Knowing the Why, Without the How

Something that I've found really empowering and affirming lately is focusing on the 'why' of what I'm looking to manifest, and leaving the 'how' to unfold in its own way. So often in business (or life) we get caught up in *how* everything is going to come our way. How am I going to make $10,000 months? How am I going to get more social media followers? How can I get more clients? How can I save enough money for our dream home? How can I be more present with my children, partner or friends?

But what if you let go of the how, and instead focused on the *why*? Why is it that you want these things to happen in your business or life? What would be different for you if you had these things? Why would it be important or feel good? Tapping into the why and purpose behind the things that you want, is so important because it drives your commitment and motivation and also gives your money a purpose.

For example, my more external why behind growing my personal brand and reaching more women with my work is to support them to release their doubts, and show up more powerfully for themselves and their business by aligning with their unique energy, story and gifts—so they can attract the impact and income they deserve. This vision fuels my passion and purpose to show up everyday with new content, support my clients and expand my reach.

My more internal why is that I want to create a full time

income on part time hours that allows me to work from home around caring for my family. By knowing that this business allows me the flexibility to leverage my impact all from a laptop, and be able to provide for my family in a way that also feels like my soul's work—is beyond motivating.

When you stick to your why and focus in on all of the reasons you want what you want and are doing what you're doing, the how takes care of itself. So often we can't predict *how* things will turn out. You may have opportunities or money come into your life in unexpected ways and could have never imagined that it would appear that way. That's why focusing on the how can actually be limiting for you, especially as it's not coming from the future version of you, and holds you to the things you expect rather than being open to things eventuating in their own way.

A perfect example of this is when a client of mine was looking to collaborate with some big name people in her industry and was getting caught up in how to contact them, who to contact, how to write an email pitch and how it would be best for them to work together. We decided to step back from this for the time being and focus her energy into sharing her gifts, talking about her story and the passion/purpose behind her brand, and showing up consistently in places where she could be seen by influential people in her industry. She then had a dream person reach out to collaborate with her on some content! During calls with me or writing in her journal or creating strategic plans, she never could have come up with this scenario playing out how it did. So when you focus in on the what and the why of what you're doing, rather than how it's all going to happen, the how sorts itself out.

All you need to do is continue to confirm why you're worthy

of the things you want, why you're here doing the things you're doing, why you're so passionate about the work that you do, and why having your desired lifestyle is so important to you. When you hold that energy and embody it, the how begins to unveil itself in ways you couldn't have planned for.

Who Are Your People?

Another important part of manifesting the future that you desire and growing your impact is to know who your people are. You've probably heard this countless times in the online business world: know who your ideal client is. And while this is important to know so that your content efforts and offers are relevant to who you want to support, this can also go a layer deeper.

We all want to belong. It's our innate instinct to do whatever we need to do to belong to a tribe and be safe. The issue that can arise with this, is it can lead you to subconsciously want to be seen and accepted by everyone. But in the business world, if you're appealing to everyone you're appealing to no one. The reason is that your messaging becomes so vague and general that people can't really relate to you or see themselves as your client. The more specific and niche you can be in what you help people with and who you help, the more you can create content and offers that speak specifically to their needs. This means being okay with the fact that not everyone is your person. Not everyone will like what you offer, and that's a *good* thing. It means nothing about your worth or capability, it just simply means that those people are not your people and it frees you up to find the ones who are.

The more steadfast you can be in knowing who you are here to support, the more you'll be able to show up for them consistently and call them into your business. This looks like knowing their common pains/struggles, the impacts of those pains/struggles in their life, why it's important to them to change their situation, the ideal things they would like to see in their life instead, and the key result or transformation that people will have by working with you. By starting to get clear on those areas, it will become more and more obvious who *your* people are and how to speak directly to them.

This also goes for your personal life. Not everyone around you is going to see your vision, in fact very few will. It's up to you to hold your vision and be unwavering in that. It's also up to you to know who your people are in your personal life. Who's got your back? Who's your support team? Who's the person you can go to when you feel fear or doubt? You may find that you also need to attract some of your people in your personal life. This could be in the form of business buddies, coaches, group program communities or friends who are more like-minded.

Surrounding yourself and attracting the right people into your business and life is a key part of calling in the results you deserve. Because they are the people that can have a direct impact on how you show up for yourself and others. As I mentioned in chapter four, not everyone will see you in your business—and that's okay. The people who will see you, like *really* see you, are the people who are ready for you and what you can offer them. Those are your people.

The Manifest-Action Mindset

I'm going to step you through my Manifest-Action Mindset Framework to help you begin...

1. *Write down everything you desire with exact clarity.*
2. *Rate your beliefs and desires out of ten.*
3. *Write down what life would like and who you'd be if you had everything you desire.*
4. *Ask for what you desire or invite it in.*
5. *Set your goals and dream building.*
6. *Remove resistance and trust in yourself and your ability.*
7. *Move towards your goal and collect evidence.*
8. *Surrender to divine timing.*

Step 1 – Write down everything you desire with exact clarity

In order to manifest and create action towards the things that you desire in life, you have to know what you actually want. How many times do you hear people say I just want to be happy, I just want to be rich or I want to start a business?

These are all typical examples of desires that are vague and wishy washy and have no way of reinforcing what you actually want. The first thing that you need to do is have full clarity and honesty with what you want in life.

Example: 'I want to be rich' vs 'I want to generate a minimum of $30,000 for my initial program launch within a fourteen day period by signing up at least 25 clients and then build on this exponentially with each relaunch of the program'.

Clarity. I know how many clients I need to acquire to reach my financial goal and can then create intentional actions combined with positive mindset strategies to manifest my goal into being.

Step 2 – Rate your beliefs out of ten

The next step is to rate the clear goals you've written out according to the following ratings:

1. How much you *want* the goal or desire to manifest in your life? (The rating is out of ten, with one being not at all and ten being more than anything else)

2. How much you *believe* that you can bring this into your life through committed action and thought? (A rating of one is no belief and a rating of ten is full belief that it can be achieved)

Now I want you to take a look at your ratings and look for any that you have rated below a seven. *I consider a rating of seven to indicate 'I want it, but I'm ok if it doesn't happen right away' or 'I want it, but I'm not too sure its going to happen for me.'*

Anything below a seven means one of three things – **it's not a clear enough goal for you to want it more, it's not something you believe enough in or it's not really a high priority desire.** So now you'll need to consider how you can bring these ratings to a seven or above. Check whether your goals are clear enough, believable enough and desirable enough.

For example, let's say my goal was to get a new black BMW SUV by the end of the year that is worth $100,000 and has space for children, a dog and camping equipment. So I might already have a car that has space for children, a dog etc, so I'm not that desperate for an upgrade. So perhaps I'll rate it as six for my level of desire. I might believe that $100,000 on a car is not realistic for me by the end of the year, so I rate it as a five for my level of belief...

So how can I raise my ratings? Well, is there a feature that I'm after that my current car doesn't have—such as automatic parking assist or reversing cameras or particular safety features for driving with children? Will this brand help me to feel more prestigious or affluent in my community? Adding more clarity to my goal here will help me to move my desire up to a seven or above.

Is there a way I can make my goal more believable? Perhaps reducing the worth of the car to $70,000 will help to raise my belief rating to an eight or nine. See how you can tinker with your goals to raise both your desire and your belief, because you want your goals to be top of mind and priority as you move forward in life.

Step 3 - Write down what life would like and who you'd be if you had everything you desire

The next step is to write down in detail what life would be like and how you'd show up if you had all of the things that you desire.

Imagining life after achieving your desires is a key part of many manifestation programs as it helps to improve your mindset, belief, neural networks and likelihood of moving towards these goals. But most importantly, it evokes one of the most important questions—your why.

Why you do and want things is so important for building your mindset and belief and improving the likelihood of moving towards your goals? If you can't see how a desire would positively impact your life or business then why even put energy into it?

The reason for wanting what you want my not be so obvious or positive and that's okay. By continually reflecting on what your life would be life, you'll keep building on your why and your clarity, belief and desire will continue to grow with it.

I also recommend practicing gratitude for the opportunity to pursue these goals or desires and manifest them into your life.

As you know, one of my desires is to start a family with my partner and one of my visions is that we will have moments in our lounge room where we cuddle up on the couch and watch our children playing and we just look at each other and smile knowing how blessed, healthy and loving our family is.

I imagine this in my mind at night and the immense happiness, fulfillment, love and connection that this would bring me and I express my gratitude for being able to have those moments with my family one day. It means so much to me and because my 'want' and 'belief' is at a ten, I then partake in the action part of manifest-action (which I'll cover) and my actions, behaviours and thoughts contribute daily to me being able to make this desire a reality and bring it into my life.

Step 4 - Ask for what you desire or invite it in

The next step is to ask for what you desire and put it out into the universe, and this can come in multiple formats.

You might choose to write a letter detailing your goals and desires and why these are important for you to achieve. You might create a vision board that you keep near your computer to reflect on. You might prey to your source (whether that's god or the universe or your higher self) requesting that you are supported to move into alignment with these desires. As this process is not just about putting your desires out there and hoping they will manifest, you also need to take reasonable actions to *tangibly* ask for what you desire.

This could look like:

- Emailing certain people and requesting their support.
- Vocalising your desires with your partner, family or friends to be accountable for their fruition.
- Creating calls to action for your business so that people know what you are asking of them, promoting and advertising yourself and your products or services.
- Sitting down with your team and asking for changes to take place.
- Putting automations or employees in place and in a sense asking for help to free you up to focus on your top priorities.

It also involves making room for what you want. It's difficult to ask for more, when you don't allow space for what is and space for more.

A reminder of some ways to create space for what you want:

- Tidy up your home, closet, desk etc, and declutter.
- Buy things that relate to what it is that you want so you're taking small steps in the right direction.
- Put intentional time into your schedule to take action steps towards your desires.
- Remove toxic friendships, connections, followers etc that pull you away from what you desire and move towards connections with more aligned people.
- Set up an environment that would easily welcome what you desire. For example, if your desire magically appeared, could you actually accommodate it or receive it?

Step 5 – Set your goals and dream building

So far we've looked at more of the mental aspects of manifesting abundance in your life including getting clear on your goals, rating your level of desire and belief and enhancing this, imagining your life if these goals manifested and why they are important to you, and asking for your goals and desires in both tangible and non-tangible ways.

Now we're going to look at the action part of the Manifest-Action Mindset, because thinking something isn't enough in itself to make it happen. Your positive mindset and unwavering belief are critical in manifesting abundance, but this needs to also combine with intentional action and behaviours that move you towards your goals.

It's no use having the desire to lose twenty-five kilograms within six months, knowing how much it will improve your life and wellbeing and then kickback on the couch with the same eating and exercise habits expecting the weight loss to manifest. Not gonna happen!

This step is about goal setting and dream building. You need to get clear on at least three actions or behaviours that you can commit to that will help to propel you closer to your goals and desires.

These actions or behaviours need to be realistic but not to the point that you limit potential growth and I recommend considering the SMART framework when planning out your action steps.

The second part of this step is called dream building and looks at ways you can begin to emulate aspects of your goal or desire and slowly start to 'build the dream.'

So let's say someone has a desire to start their own fashion business in the next year and launch a line of fifteen outfits for the spring season. Part of their dream building might include booking a venue months in advance for their fashion show, or purchasing and wearing an expensive fashion garment that they know they would wear if they already had a successful fashion business.

You can be creative with your dream building and it doesn't have to involve a lot of money. You'll also find a section in your workbook where you can come up with some ideas for dream building for each of your goals or desires.

Step 6 – Remove resistance and trust in yourself

The next step is to remove resistance and trust in yourself and your ability. This step is all about maintaining your Manifest-Action Mindset and reinforcing the steps you've already covered regularly so that your mindset remains focused on growth, belief and the positive outcomes that your desires would bring you.

If things aren't showing up immediately it can be easy to get discouraged and consciously or subconsciously resist the process. You might consider giving up on your goals or even begin sabotaging them or gathering evidence to why they can't happen for you.

When you feel this resistance coming up, it's important to make use of the mindset tools that you have developed previously. Move back across previous steps to refocus on why you had these desires or goals in the first place and spend some time imagining what your life would look like to achieve these things.

You may need to rewrite some of your actions to be more aligned with where you are currently at or to adapt to any challenges or life changes that have presented.

In order to embrace the Manifest-Action Mindset and bring about your goals and desires, you need to ultimately trust and believe in yourself and your ability to achieve.

Moving through any limiting beliefs, stories or setbacks is paramount to being able to manifest abundance in your life and I recommend reviewing lessons from the previous modules to support you to manage any resistance that is popping up.

Step 7 – Move towards your goal and collect evidence

The final step is to continue moving towards your goal and collect evidence along the way. Focus on the actions that you have developed for your goals and continue to envisage what your life would be like once you achieve your goals.

By acknowledging that there may be days where setbacks arise or you encounter resistance, you can take some time out to reflect on your progress so far and continue moving forward even if the movement you make feels less than the day before.

A key part of moving forward is to also collect evidence of how you are progressing towards your future desires. This involves celebrating the small wins along the way and reflecting on or documenting ways that you have progressed at least every week. I recommend keeping a positivity journal that you specifically document any small wins, positive feedback or progress.

This will trigger your Reticular Activating System and help you to keep momentum and remain focused on your actions so that you have a higher likelihood of manifesting your desires. Your Reticular Activaiting System is the part of your brain that filters essential information into your consciousness and is the reason you'll suddenly buy a new car and then see that model on the road constantly. It's the notion of 'what you focus on expands' and is a powerful tool in manifesting because your brain can't decifer whether what you're focused on is real or illusion. Focus on what you do want, so you can attract it into your consciousness.

Acting as If

Earlier on in this book, I wrote about stepping into the new you and how to take proactive steps to become the person you envisage with powerful routines and habits. This becomes even more important as you move into manifesting what is it that you want and being able to call in new ways of being into your life.

There might be simple changes that you can start to make *now,* that allow you to start acting like the person you want to be. It doesn't all just click one day and you become a new person. It starts now, with micro habits and conscious decisions to *show up* differently. What can you do *today* to start showing up as the person you want to be? What can you do to call in the results that you desire in your business and life?

This might include adding or making changes such as:

- A Supportive Daily Routine
- Gratitude Practice
- Journaling
- Visualisation/Vision Boards/Morning Manifesto
- Affirmations
- Commit to One Key Weekly Change—Be at my kids sports practice, yoga class, dinner at a restaurant, spray tan, video content, no laptop on Saturdays etc.

Who is the future you? Give her a name. Own her in the present. Let her be your becoming.

Crafting Your Ideal Life

There needs to be a commitment to the life that you want to create and that it doesn't have to be in the far off future. You can get started right now with small things that take you closer to the person you want to show up as and the life that you want to lead.

Real change amalgamates from small actions that combine. I used to provide counselling for clients with drug and alcohol issues and we never took the cold turkey approach. We would come up with a plan together for behaviour change that aligned with their goals and their level of dependency, and they would commit to micro changes (such as reduce by one glass of wine per week or no alcohol on Sundays etc.) Once those habits became ingrained we would move to add more changes, including mindset/trauma support, until they we're at a point where they had made positive changes to their addiction.

It all starts with a decision. Your ideal life isn't just sitting in the clouds waiting for you. Even if you believe in fate or that your destiny is pre-determined, it requires action and intention on your part to allow the pieces of your life to fall into place. We have to call it in. We have to be open to receiving what it is that we want and be receptive to how it unfolds. It may not happen exactly how you'd planned in your head, but it may happen in a way that's better than you could have ever imagined.

Intuitive Insights

1. *What do you want to manifest in your business and life?*
2. *What did you uncover by working through the Manifest-Action Mindset for yourself?*
3. *What can you do this week to begin aligning with your goals and calling them into being?*
4. *How does your routine need to change to accommodate your goals and how you want to show up?*

10

Sustainable Supports

'No business is an island,' this is a saying that I have continually reminded myself of over the years of running my businesses. In the early days of growing our skincare brand, it really was just my partner and I against the world.

We didn't have anyone helping us, we didn't have anyone coaching us, we didn't have anyone who really knew what it was like.

The many days where I commuted forty-five minutes to the city, worked for eight hours, then commuted home and went straight into side hustle mode for another three to four hours... for years.

The weekends that were spent on marketing, accounting and fulfillment while my friends were out enjoying themselves.

The sacrifices of things like buying a house and starting a family in my twenties, because we wanted to invest our time and money into business growth and make time for following our passions.

I taught myself how to build websites, how to design graphics, how to run Facebook Ads and how to manage wholesalers and staff. You could say we were the definition of self-made, because we were turning over multi-six figures years in sales with very little support.

But as time went on and our brand became more sought after, I realised how much we did need to lean on both personal and professional supports to help us to continue achieving our goals.

Even within my personal brand, although it's me at the helm, I know that I have needed to surround myself with the right supports to help me to achieve what I can't do alone.

After my quarter-life breakdown moment, I made a promise to myself that I wouldn't keep sacrificing my wellbeing, relationships and life goals in pursuit of business success (this later became the motto behind my entrepreneurship). But that meant leaning on supports in all of the varied ways, so that I could continue to show up for myself, those close to me, and my clients/audience.

For me, support has always meant more than just the people around me. It's first and foremost how I support myself—from a physical, mental, emotional, social and spiritual perspective. Because if I can't show up and support myself, it's unfair for me to expect others around me to be the ones holding things together.

It then means looking at the people you're surrounding yourself with. How do they make you feel? Do they support you in your goals? Do they offer support in the ways that you need it? Sometimes we can keep people in our circle because of how long we've known them, or because it feels egotistical to admit that you're on different paths, but just like knowing when a romantic partnership is no longer serving you, you also need to know when friend or family relationships aren't aligned anymore.

Then finally, support also means the environment that you place yourself in to do the work that you do. Do you have a dedicated space where you do your best work? Do you have a team or assistant supporting you with tasks that dim your light? Have you invested in software or processes to help you to elevate your business and work smarter, not harder?

The success of your business, and your ability to uphold your energy and shine your light, comes from being able to create a supportive and effective environment in both your business and your life.

As I moved into this year and started my realignment with the kind of work I wanted to be doing within this personal brand, I needed to take another look at my support system.

I was going to be moving through big changes, letting go of hours of work, going through a period where I may not bring in clients, and rebuilding from the foundations. I knew the people around me were supportive of my endeavours and believed in me and what I could achieve, so it was more about the support I was showing myself.

As an INFJ Personality Type (Myers Briggs Personality Types), I'm naturally introverted, deep thinking and empathetic. I've never been the life of the party, the girl who lights up the room, or the girl who everybody seems to love.

I've never been surrounded by big groups of friends and always struggled to meet business buddies that stuck around.

I don't ooze positive, bubbly, smiling energy and I often have to mentally prepare for parties or gatherings where I have to engage in small talk or act overly extroverted.

My energy easily gets drained when I'm showing up publicly or have too many things to do at once.

For a long time I thought this was a character flaw, especially as the majority of people in my life are extroverts. But I've come to realise that I don't need to be the extroverted #bossgirl to be successful and the more that I stay true to myself and my needs, the better I can sustain my energy and continue to show up and share my light.

At the start of the year I had such a strong vision of the woman and mother I wanted to be, and I knew that throughout most of last year, I hadn't been showing up as her. I envisioned a confident, put-together, positive, ambitious and carefree woman who had specific business goals and showed up daily to create content and serve her clients.

She balanced business and home life with ease and everything and everyone had a share of time and attention. She was *Overflowing Sienna*. But as the majority of my days throughout a global pandemic had been spent in leggings and a messy bun with a total of around thirty days where I wore makeup, I knew there was some work to do.

I committed to new habits of how I would show up for myself and my life if I was already this woman. I purchased an exercise program membership and committed to stop neglecting my physical fitness. I purchased new work clothes and makeup and committed to dressing well and presenting myself as if I was off to work at a corporate job each day. I purchased self-care items like a new journal, bath salts, candles and creative activities to commit to giving myself down time and reflection time. I committed to dropping into a state of flow and belief regarding my conception journey. I invested in software, training and a co-working space that would support me to bring my new aligned business vision to life. I overhauled my weekly routine and batched tasks and objectives into clear days and time-slots so I could show up with full attention and be more productive.

All of these things formed part of my support system and didn't involve being reliant on anyone else but myself. I knew that I needed to show up for myself, before I could expect others to show up for me. If I didn't approach my business with confidence and belief, how could I expect others to show confidence and belief in it?

You can't expect any one person to be your go-to support for all things in your life. When you can have different people in your support network that have different skills, insights or advice for your different needs, it lessens the burden on others to be all things to you.

Furthermore, I realised over the years that often you need to be your own go-to for addressing your needs and seeking answers because the majority of the time you're the one who knows you best. That's when you really craft an intuitive impact.

This year feels like it's going to be full of big, bold energy where we'll start to really shift into alignment with what lights us up and go after our inspired, intuitive goals.

Maybe you feel it too?

If so, I hope that this book serves as a guide to taking the first steps, and that this chapter supports you to better support yourself throughout your up-level.

Releasing the Guilt

Leaning on additional supports and systems within your business can sometimes come with a dose of guilt or perceived weakness. But getting the right supports and systems in place to avoid burnout and grow your business in a sustainable way is **anything but weak.** It's a sign that you know how to leverage resources to achieve results.

Releasing the guilt is a process that takes conscious practice, but will allow you to more fully step into growing your personal brand and impact.

Who am I to be out at brunch while others are working?
Who am I to make money while I sleep?
Who am I to be able to travel and take my business with me in a laptop?

It's an adjustment to a new way of working, but as more and more people take advantage of the opportunities to leverage their time, energy and money, it will become easier to adjust to working smarter, not harder.

Here's what I recommend to help release any guilt associated with getting support so you can do less work and make more money within your business:

- Truly believe that hard work doesn't equal success.
- Understand that technology has been created for us to simplify our lives.
- Ask yourself if you had time and money for what matters most to you, would it be worth it? Generally it's a yes.

- Focus on quality of work over quantity of work—you can achieve the same client results & outcomes by leveraging online systems and supports.
- Working less doesn't mean you're less committed to your dreams.
- Consider where the guilt is coming from and work on addressing this—like others' expectations of you.

No Business is an Island

Even as a solo business owner, no business is an island. There are a range of supports that business owners lean on to create and grow their businesses.

Even as a solo operator, that will only get you so far before it feels as though you're burning out doing everything yourself. *In order to surpass multiple six figures – seven figures you need additional support.*

This comes in the form of:

- Personal Supports
- Professional Supports (People)
- Professional Supports (Technology)

Supporting Yourself

Sometimes you may need to lean on support from others because you're not currently in a position to support yourself. This is nothing to be ashamed of and so important that you know how and when to ask for help when you need it. So many women (and men) suffer in silence, not willing to ask for support or guidance with their challenges. As we know, not seeking support for yourself can lead to worsening mental health, physical illness or more tragic consequences. There is always someone around you who is willing to support you, even when you think there is no one.

I'm so passionate about highlighting mental health in business, because we're so often fed the message that in order to have success we have to suck it up or there's no room for emotions. I think these expectations place so much unnecassary pressure on business owners to do things on their own and avoid seeking support, often at their own detriment.

On top of seeking support from others when needed, you can also take steps to better support yourself each day. It can be challenging over time to expect others to give to you, what you're not giving to yourself. If you want clients who follow their health plan, or pay you on time, or work on enhancing their mindset...then you need to be embodying these things in your own life.

You need to be your own best client, to attract more of the same into your world. This can again look like daily routines, rituals or habits that we've covered in other chapters to allow you to better support your own wellbeing, relationship and life goals and create a solid support framework within yourself.

When you know you can rely on yourself as a core source of support, it builds trust and confidence in your ability to show up for yourself and others in a more powerful way.

Building Personal Supports

Often your ability to start and grow your own business, comes with the support of others around you. This could include your extended family, partner, children, friends, community or even in some cases support from your current employment.

Businesses can often require sacrifices, accommodations and patience from more than just the business owner and that's why your personal support network is so important.

Types of personal supports:

- Extended family
- Partner
- Friends
- Previous Colleagues
- Community Groups
- Business Networks

If you feel like you're lacking personal supports, I recommend considering how you can surround yourself with more supportive people who understand your goals. This could include attending local business workshops, business Facebook groups, connecting with like-minded people on social media, or joining online coaching programs that foster community.

Challenging Conversations

There can be times when people in your life may not understand your vision or goals and challenge how you're spending your time, money or attention. Sometimes it becomes clear who you can and cannot talk about your business with and it may be worth finding alternative supports where you feel open to sharing about your business journey.

If you do find yourself in a challenging conversation around your business, here are some tips that I recommend:

1. **Explain the 'why' behind your business and the reason behind pursuing your business or investing your time/money in a particular pursuit in a way that is a mutual goal.** *Is it to provide more financial freedom for your family? Is it to allow you to travel without restriction?*
2. **Help the person to understand the return on investment or benefits.** *What will this opportunity open up for you? What will it teach you to do or how will it create a chance to build your personal brand or get in-front of clients?*
3. **Understand that you don't need permission from others to pursue your dreams.** *Sometimes you might be your only cheerleader and results will speak volumes to any nay-sayers.*
4. **Explain your version of success and how that may not be the 'norm' but can you have their support in giving it a try.** *How can you help them to view business in a different way?*

Building Professional Supports

Supporting yourself behind the scenes of your business can also be enhanced with professional supports in the form of both people and technology.

Professional supports can help with the day to day running of your business and allow you to focus on the biggest impact and income generating tasks, without getting bogged down in low level tasks.

Types of professional supports:

- Freelancers / Contractors
- Home Support (Daycare, Nanny, Cleaner, Handyman, Dog Walker etc)
- Virtual Team
- Employees
- Mentor / Coach
- Technology (Automations, Systems, Software, Programs, Communities)

You can hire professional supports in your local area or by using websites dedicated to providing business owners with support:

- Upwork.com
- Freelancer.com
- Task Rabbit
- Air Tasker
- Job websites

Looking at Support Differently

Money vs Time

When you consider improving your personal or professional supports, it's important to remind yourself of the money vs time debate. What would it be worth to you to free up one hour of cleaning to focus on attracting new clients into your business? If each client who signs up for your service is worth $1000, then paying a cleaner $40 for one hour seems well worth the investment.

If investing in additional supports frees up your precious time and energy to create bigger results in your business, then it ends up paying for itself.

Opportunity Cost

Another way to look at the money vs time consideration is by determining the opportunity cost.

What is the cost of spending your time doing everything yourself?

Does it pull you away from promoting your content? Does it pull you away from being with your family? Does it pull you away from recharging your energy?

If the 'cost' of spending time on tasks that don't need to be done by you is too high, then you might like to look at how you can delete, delegate or digitise them.

Releasing Control

A common thing that I hear from business owners when it comes to getting support with tasks is 'It's easier to just do it myself' or 'They'll never do it as well as me.' This may be true... at least in the beginning. But it's your job to teach and empower your supports to do the job to a similar standard as you with workflows, positive feedback and structured templates.

I often suggest here to be hiring people who are *more* effective at the task than you. Hire people who are passionate about the task that you need support with and it's likely they may even do a *better* job than you!

When it comes to getting support from others, I also work off an 80% rule.

If the task completed is at least 80% as good as what I would achieve by doing it myself, then I am happy. I can then work on getting better outcomes in the future. If you are unable to loosen the grip, it will be difficult to scale your business beyond your own capacity over time. Even with a fully automated online business model or service programs, there will come a time when you'll need additional support as you grow.

Energetic Support

Something that's often not considered when it comes to supporting yourself is the role that your energy plays with your productivity, commitment and results.

Your daily routine (including any specific morning routine and/or evening routine) is actually a vital part of your support plan. If you're not structuring your day in a way that works in with your own energy levels, rhythms, and cycles then it can mean you're working against flow and could be scheduling work tasks at times that end up leaving you depleted.

When I overhauled my routine to provide energetic support throughout my week, it made such a huge difference to how I showed up each day and lead to far more effective work output and results.

Prior to overhauling my weekly routine and schedule, I was jumping from task to task like they were hot coals. I'd have multiple tasks on the go at once (sometimes for multiple businesses) and would usually do tasks based on what popped up in the moment. Ever had an email come through that's lead you down a rabbit hole for an hour and pulled you away from what you were actually doing?

I learnt the power of batching my work days and work tasks, but then took it one level deeper than many time management books or productivity coaches talk about, and structured everything in accordance with my energy on any given day or week.

There are a number of different energy considerations when it comes to structuring your schedule, which I'll detail below. This is not about smashing down your fifth coffee for the day until you feel like an energizer bunny and forcing yourself to complete tasks. This is about aligning with the different aspects of your energy body and creating a feeling of flow in your day and week. Take it from me, someone who hasn't been drinking coffee for over twelve months!

Energy Levels - Physical

This type of energy is probably the one you're more familiar with and refers to your physical energy levels, such as your level of fatigue/exhaustion/motivation/focus.

This type of energy is the one coming through when you're ready to hit the ground running on a Monday morning with your weekly goals, or ready to take a snooze and have a chocolate bar by 3 p.m.

It's the energy that categorises you as an early bird, night owl—or a permanently exhausted pigeon!

Whether you realise it or not, your physical energy levels can have a big impact on how productive you are during the day.

If you're scheduling important tasks for first thing in the morning, when you *know* it takes you until 10 a.m. to even wake up to the day, then you're probably not going to be as effective with that task compared to if it was scheduled after lunch time.

Similarly, if you've often got client calls or tasks where you need to be 'on the ball' and you're scheduling these on Friday afternoons when you know you're mentally winding down for the week, then that's not all that helpful either.

When I started batching and scheduling tasks in accordance with my energy levels, it made such a huge difference to my motivation and focus while completing those tasks. The simplest way to address this in your schedule, is to break down your day into two hour increments and rate your energy/focus level in those blocks as low, medium or high.

I'm not a morning person, so on any typical day I don't usually hit my stride until about 10 a.m.-1 p.m. Then by 3-5 p.m. I usually go through a low energy period before perking up again after dinner from around 8-10 p.m.

So when it comes to scheduling tasks for the week ahead, I'll align high focus tasks like client calls/podcast episodes/creating content between 10 a.m.-1 p.m. or 8-10 p.m., if I choose to work late. I'll schedule low focus and menial tasks like answering emails/posting content/accounting etc, during the 2-5 p.m. time slot where less of my energy is required.

You can also zoom out and do this from more of a weekly perspective and take note of your energy across a week. By Thursday and Friday I'm usually more depleted so I try to schedule more 'behind the scenes' tasks on those days so I don't need to show up in my full energy.

Energy Levels - Spiritual

Another aspect of your energy is your spiritual energy. This level of energy comes from feeling like you're doing purposeful work, you're aligned in business and life, you're creating an impact or legacy, and feeling on path with your direction.

Have you ever had moments where you've felt confused with your direction or perhaps like you're not fully aligned with the work you're meant to be doing in the world—and it's a complete energy suck?

No matter how many coffees you drink or walks you take, you just can't seem to get yourself into a zone where you can do the work?

I've definitely been there before, especially over the last few months of last year. I knew that my energetic alignment was off and I needed to overhaul how I was structuring my routines and schedule so that I felt a sense of flow, vibrancy and purpose.

Apart from aligning fully with your purpose, which we cover throughout this book...one of the simplest ways to address your energy from a more spiritual and soul perspective is with daily/weekly rituals that fill your cup and recharge your energy. This could look like a structured morning and/or evening routine, or it could be a collection of go-to rituals that you sprinkle into your day as needed.

I personally prefer to have a more ad-hoc approach to this process because it can become really easy to get stuck in the thought that you *must* do your morning routine every day without fail or your whole day is ruined—and it can become something that does the opposite of improving your vibe.

Rituals might include things like a nice breakfast and beverage without looking at your phone, a meditation practice, a short break in the sun, a walk with a friend or pet, playing some upbeat or relaxing music, turning your phone to airplane mode, journalling or reading.

It's up to you to determine what kind of habits, rituals or hobbies light you up and recharge your energy and then commit to integrating them into your day or week, or as needed. If you're constantly doing tasks that drain your energy and forgetting to recharge that energy, it's a surefire route to burnout.

As an introvert, I have to be very mindful of my energy levels in this way. If I'm doing too much 'front of stage' work in one day or week such as client calls, group coaching, podcast episodes and content creation, I can easily become drained.

So a big part of scheduling my week is ensuring that these types of tasks are not only in an appropriate time slot based on my physical energy, but are also spread out accordingly so I can be sure to recharge in between.

Natural Cycles

Another consideration that may or may not be important for you when creating a supportive schedule, is the natural cycles that we experience.

This may be your menstrual cycle, the moon cycles or the cycles of seasons. You may be someone who has a change in energy or mood depending on where you are at in your menstrual cycle, or you may find that you're impacted by the change in the moon, or that you're more motivated in summer and more low on energy and drive in the winter.

These changes with the natural cycles around you can also be considered when it comes to structuring your schedule and on a larger scale, your goals. If you can predict times when you're going to be less able to show up in your business or for others, you can schedule important tasks and goals in your business around this knowledge rather than forcing yourself to do the work when you're not at your optimal.

My motivation and energy can often impacted by the weather. When it's sunny and warm I feel far more in my element than when it's cold and rainy. Because of this, I make an effort to get outside more when the weather is better and take breaks to sit out in the sunshine. When the weather is cold or gloomy, I make an effort to enhance the environment around me with cosy blankets, warm cups of tea, warm baths, and candles so that I can work on boosting my energy despite what the weather is like.

Do what works for you, but know that you get to dictate your schedule in a way that suits you and feels more aligned so that you're *supporting* your results, rather than *forcing* your results.

Sand, Pebbles and Rocks

A fantastic analogy that I learnt via Steph Crowder (Business Strategist and Podcaster) was the sand, pebbles and rocks analogy. This is a scheduling tool that can support you to craft a more intentional week.

Rocks - Most important, non-negotiable tasks like meetings, client calls, appointments, work hours (if you have another job), school pick up time etc.

Pebbles - Tasks that don't have a set deadline or time-slot and are things that you're working on in your business or life but if there is no real consequence if it's not completed like blog posts, accounting reports, painting the garage, catching up with a friend, setting up a new web page etc.

Sand - Low level menial tasks like following up emails, responding to social media messages, doing the groceries, mowing the lawn etc.

Many people plan their week by prioritising the sand, then the pebbles, then the rocks. The problem with this is that if you imagine a jar, the sand fills up the majority of the jar and then you're left trying to squish in the pebbles and rocks.

The alternative to this is to plan your week by prioritising the rocks, then the pebbles, then the sand. This means that the most important rocks are going into your jar first (tasks in your schedule), then the pebbles will slot in around that, and then the sand will naturally glide in and fall into the blank spaces. This way, you ensure that you're making time for not only the important tasks but also the business/life growth tasks that can often be neglected due to lack of time, because the 'sand' takes over.

I've found this a really helpful way of planning out my

schedule with a combination of the above considerations, and ensures that I end up (for the most part) with a schedule that includes important business and life tasks in alignment with my different levels of energy and cycles. It's allowed me to ensure that I prioritise business growth activities like social media content, podcast episodes, and creating offers while still making time for important events or commitments in my personal life—without getting stuck always doing the 'busy' work. Overhauling your schedule in this way may just be the most supportive thing you could do for yourself, and if often not even a consideration for most business owners.

Intuitive Insights

1. *What personal, professional or technological supports do you need to lean on in order to show up as your best in business?*
2. *What emotions come up as you consider outsourcing personal or professional tasks? What is behind that emotion and how can you release it?*
3. *How do you need to change your relationship with money vs time?*
4. *What processes or procedures can you create to allow you to let go and outsource tasks to others in a way that feels manageable?*

11

Your Alignment Plan

'If it doesn't feel good, what's the point?!' I thought to myself as I started making plans for February and beyond.

It felt like I was hitting this huge metaphorical reset button and stepping into an upgraded version of myself. My energy and vibe felt so different—in a good way.

Within days, I had the vision for this book and my new coaching programs mapped out. It felt so clear and like it had come purely from my own inner knowing of how I wanted to show up and serve my audience. There were no strict goals, no outside influences, no timelines, and no expectations on how it would all unfold. There was simply what I wanted to create in the world.

My alignment plan was simple:
- Write and publish this book within three months.
- Create a transformational coaching program to be a sup-

portive container for those who want to dive deeper into implementing what this book covers and step into more inner power, capacity & impact—without the self-sacrifice, content hamster wheel, or endless to-do list.
- Show up as the woman I wanted to be: confident, well-presented, patient, disciplined, trusting, intuitively inspired.
- Let go of the desperate energy and timeline to becoming a mother, and simply show up for it and surrender to the outcomes.

As the end of the month rolled in, I felt so positive about my direction. I was fully embracing the present moment with the belief that all that I wanted to manifest would show itself in the right timing for me.

And on the final day of the month—the 28th February—sitting in the bathroom at 7 a.m. I called in one of the points on my alignment plan...there were finally two solid lines on my pregnancy test!

In that moment, I knew that I was on the right path. I knew that everything I'd been through up until that moment, was meant for me. I needed to learn the lessons to eliminate the things that hadn't been working for me.

Time stood still as I ran out to Chris crying my eyes out to tell him we were having a baby. I ugly cried for a good hour and felt all of the months of waiting and wishing ooze out of me. This was our rainbow baby and I had never felt more grateful and ready for something in my whole life. Just one day prior I had shared a photo on my Instagram of me crying to normalise that not everything is always sunshine and butterflies in business or life. In the days leading up to taking the pregnancy test, I had this strange sense of calm but was also emotional about the prospect of another negative test. I wasn't expecting a result either way and it felt so serendipitous that the month I released was the month I received.

I truly believe that the shifts I made in my business and life that month allowed me to step into a space of flow where I could open up to conceive. And up until that point it involved a process of conquering the past, embracing the present and then manifesting the future.

As the next month unfolded and I continued to write this book, I maintained the energy of the previous month. I put my intentions out into the world and showed up for them in the way that I wanted to and then let go of the outcomes. The timelines looked a little different as I navigated pregnancy fatigue and nausea, but I stayed true to my intentions.

At the beginning of February (before I knew I was pregnant) I picked out a random crystal from a mixed bag that I purchased. It was an orange translucent crystal which I worked out to be citrine. Citrine is a crystal associated with abundance and positive energy, but ironically it is also one of the birthstones of November. I couldn't help but see it as a sign, knowing that if we were to successfully conceive that month, then we would be having a November baby.

Each evening, I held the crystal and meditated about the things I wanted to manifest into my life, bringing positive and abundant energy into my body and mind. As our ultrasound date lingered, I moved deeper into focusing on trusting my body to create life and that I was equipped to handle whatever came my way. I visualised my womb space nourishing and nurturing a baby and channeled love and life there.

As the days leading up to our first ultrasound came closer, I could feel the nervous energy and trauma from my miscarriage creeping in. But instead of ignoring it, I leaned into it and acknowledged that it was inevitable that these feelings would arise but that my experience last time was not going to be my experience this time. Your past does not equal your future.

To our absolute delight, on ultrasound day we saw our precious little jellybean wiggling around with a strong heartbeat—and in that moment my whole world felt complete and everything I'd been working towards up until that moment felt perfectly aligned...

Letter To My Baby

You were the one thing I couldn't click my fingers and get. That I couldn't pay someone to make happen. That I couldn't get from a book. You were everything I wanted and you showed me that in order to have it, I had to let go and surrender to not knowing when or how it would happen—but that it would.

You showed me that the same is true in business. That by trusting that the things I want will come to me, even when I don't know how or when, they will show up for me when I firstly show up for them.

All I have to do is show up for what I desire and be me. Connect to the energy of what I want and declare that 'I am here for it, however it comes!'. That's when you create results.

Balancing Business and Life

One thing that was so apparent to me going through my early struggles in business and the growth of my podcast and visibility, was the importance of creating a sense of balance between business and life. Balance is a word that's not always easy to achieve and sometimes it's something that people don't want to achieve as they lean into their passion areas.

But as someone who doesn't benefit from being 'all in' in just business or 'all in' in just life, I need to find that balance between the two. My business and work ethic thrive off feeling healthy, whole and fulfilled in my personal life and my wellbeing, energy management, and ability to give to others all thrives off how I structure my business.

If you're similar to me and know that you need to be giving attention to many aspects of your life in a way that feels manageable, then it can be done. You don't need to choose one or the other like we're often lead to believe as women. You don't need to have a thriving business *or* be an attentive mother. You don't need to have a full-time business/corporate path *or* have your own business. You don't need to have a successful business at the expense of successful relationships with others. When you choose to give time and energy to the things that matter most to you, you can find a way for them to all intersect and co-exist harmoniously.

Yes there will be periods when one priority takes up more time and energy than others, such as when your child is unwell or you have a big business launch coming up. But you can account for these ebbs and flows, and bring things back to a level of homeostasis in between.

So how do you balance business and life? I recommend working out your non-negotiables and what things you are and aren't willing to prioritise in the pursuit of your goals. For example, are you willing to reduce some time spent with your children and organise child-care so you can spend some solid hours on your business? Are you willing to forgo some of your sleep or relaxation time to work late on your business? Are you willing to delay a business project/task so you can get breakfast on the weekend with your friends? Are you willing to have your partner or supports take charge of some of your responsibilities so you can spend time on your own self-care or enjoyable activities?

When you're clear on the kind of schedule and priorities you want to upkeep, you can begin to plan out your week or month in a way that allows these priorities to co-exist. But this also needs to be paired with some grace and lowering of your standards when necessary. For example, can the dishes sit overnight so you can finish that work task? Can you hire a cleaner to free up a few hours to do something that's a higher priority? Can you hit publish on that blog or video without it being 100% perfect? Can you spend thirty minutes scrolling on Instagram to diffuse and not have it lead to guilt?

At the end of the day, life happens and as much as we work to control it there will be times where things don't go to plan and we need to instill some grace and compassion into our situation. You're doing the best you can, and the way you manage your time and energy in accordance with your highest priorities is what will allow you to feel more balanced and fulfilled across multiple aspects of your life.

Balancing Mind, Body and Soul

While you might have a good handle on balancing all of the 'external' stuff, when it comes to your internal situation things might be a little more chaotic. As I mentioned in Chapter one, one of the terms that has become a topic of discussion lately, especially for woman, is the notion of the mental load. When you're keeping track of all the things that need to get done, often inside your head, it can be exhausting. Taking the kids to soccer practice, remembering to buy more apples, feeding the dog, calling the insurance company about your rates, buying a card for your dad's birthday, sending off that work email, putting the washing in the dryer before it sits wet all day, following up with a client, booking that yoga class and so on. It's no wonder we can often feel like our minds are full of a never ending to-do list and it's hard to switch off. Responsibilities and errands will always be a part of life as an adult, but there are ways to reduce the load that you may be currently feeling.

One of the things that I find crucial to reducing my own mental load is getting it all out of my head. I use the calendar on my phone to set up my weekly schedule and I insert errands and tasks that I need to do into my calendar with their own time slot. What's important about this is that I'm not just writing a long to-do list that becomes overwhelming in itself. I'm intentionally curating when I will make time for those tasks and how I can integrate them into my week so that the load feels less heavy. For example, if I need to buy any grocery items I'll wait until I'm already going somewhere where there is a grocery store or I will find another task to combine with having to go to the grocery store. If I need to make a bunch of calls

I'll set aside an hour for calls so I don't end up doing them at random times and get stuck on hold, or better yet, I will make calls while I'm driving to maximise my time.

Another important part of reducing the mental load is looking at where you can delegate or delete tasks. Are there things you're doing just because you think you 'should' be but you actually don't enjoy it? Are there tasks you're claiming as your own when your partner or children could be taking those on? Are you maintaining high expectations of how things need to be done so that there's no other choice but for you to do it?

Women can do anything, but they can't do everything. There needs to be some fairness in how you structure your responsibilities and what you choose to take on. Women have been conditioned to feel like it's their job to maintain the household and manage the children, but if you're finding it too much or also running a business then perhaps there needs to be a discussion with the other supports in your life about how to level out the load.

Other ways to balance your energy body and mind is to participate in any activities or practices that fill your cup and allow you to switch off. This could be meditation, yoga, painting, writing, cooking, walking, singing, reading, or anything else that revitalises you and allows you to continue to give from a space of overflowing energy.

Managing Expectations

As I mentioned earlier, life happens and sometimes our best laid plans don't go the way we hoped. I found myself in a forcing energy for five months, expecting certain things to happen instead of allowing them to happen. The energetic exchange is so different. It's only natural to have expectations, especially when we're always told in business to have clear goals and clarity with our vision. But there can be clarity in your goals and unwavering belief in yourself, without being pinned to a specific result. Often when we have set expectations on how things will go, that is when we become most disappointed.

One of my clients was struggling with how things were unfolding for her and one of the things she kept saying was, 'This isn't what I expected to happen,' and that was the problem. She was so set on things unfolding in a certain way— of having a specific number of clients, of having immediate results, of people saying and doing certain things, that when it didn't happen that way, she was negatively impacted. Letting go of your expectations can often be a very freeing experience. You're no longer caught up in controlling how things go and setting yourself up for disappointment if it goes a different way. You can take steps towards goals and plans in your business, but then let go of the 'how.' You can commit to allowing things to unfold however they will and also opening up to them unfolding in a way you might not be able to comprehend.

When I finally let go of the expectation that I would get pregnant and released to the timeline that was out of my control, it was the month I got pregnant. I truly believe that I needed this experience to teach myself about the power of letting go and surrendering to the timing of our lives. While it wasn't a business-related lesson, I can see wholeheartedly how it was also teaching be about fully trusting and believing in myself within business and that things would unfold in their own way as long as I stayed committed.

Mantra - I allow things to unfold in their own way and open myself up to receiving the results I am after, or something better, in its own timing.

When It Doesn't Go to Plan

I can't talk about managing your expectations without also talking about when things don't go to plan. It's inevitable in life that there will be times when things don't work out the way you hope. It's happened to me so many times in business and life, sometimes leading me to want to give up on whatever it is I'm working towards.

But when you give up on what you want, you'll end up getting nothing anyway so I'm a big believer of continuing to try, even in the face of failure or adversity. In the moment it can be hard to see what the trials and tribulations of our life can teach us, and perhaps you won't be able to see the lessons for some time, but our failures can be our greatest teachers and healers.

One of the core characteristics of an entrepreneur is their ability to bounce back and pivot along the way. Many businesses fail in the early years because the owner is often met with adversity that they're unable or unwilling to overcome. If you can dig deep in those moments and not let it mean anything about you personally, you'll rise up and claim the results that you *so* deserve.

It might mean that you need to change your approach slightly, or align deeper with your vision, or start something from scratch—but when you know you're on track with fulfilling your passion and purpose, then moving forward becomes the only option. If you let it all go at the first sign of a mistake or set back, how would you feel in five years' time? Not living to your full potential can be one of the most painful regrets of the dying, so how can you see the mistakes along the way as stepping stones to your highest potential?

Mantra - *You never know what tomorrow will bring.*

Be Willing to Be Wrong

One of the key parts of embracing your intuition more in business and life beyond just tuning inward is willing to be wrong. There may be many times where you have an intuitive message drop in, a gut feeling or a undeniable urge to do something and you hold yourself back out of fear of making a wrong decision or failing. Embracing your intuition can't work if you only *think* the things and never actually *do* them.

So a big part of manifesting the things you want from an aligned and intuitive perspective is to be willing to take action on your ideas and have them not work out or be the wrong decision. That doesn't mean you're a failure or not cut out for the things you want, it just means you learn what doesn't work and can redirect to what's next.

The people who get results in business are the ones who are willing to put themselves out there and take messy action without caring what the outcome is. So have you been holding yourself back from doing the things that your heart is calling you to do, out of fear of being wrong or having it not work out?

It's time to start leaning into putting those smaller intuitive hits into action and allowing yourself to learn and grow along the way. Most of my biggest business learnings have come from making mistakes and having things not work or turn out well. The knowledge you gain is actually golden!

Creating Your Alignment Plan

What would your business and life look like if it felt perfectly aligned and in flow? What would you be doing each day? What results would you be getting?

Part of manifesting the future and calling in the things you want in your business and life is being conscious of exactly what those things are. If you don't know what you want, how can you know when you get it? If you don't know what feels good, how can you find joy in your business? If you don't know your direction with clarity, how can it manifest for you?

My six phase Intuitive Impact Approach is the foundation of my group and private coaching programs. You're lovingly guided through creating and implementing your own unique Business Alignment Plan that clarifies each phase of the approach for your situation, so you can show up more powerfully and claim the stand-out, sold-out and scalable impact that I *know* is possible for you.

In this section, I've outlined the six phases and the key areas of focus that fall under each phase. You may like to brainstorm how these focus areas could be implemented into your own business and life, or consider getting some guidance from me so I can put my eyes on your situation and support you to construct a clear and comprehensive plan.

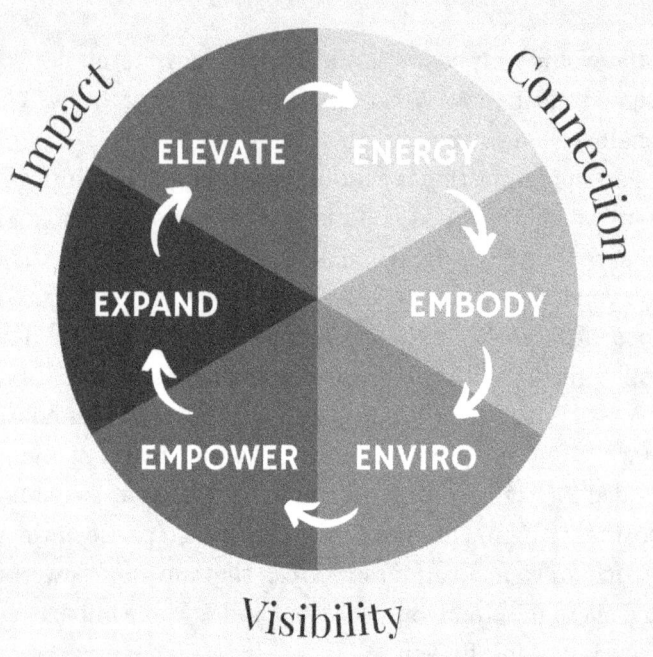

Phase 1 - Connection

Energy - Stop over-giving and start honouring and amplifying your energy

- Identifying your Business Energy Archetype and unique energy needs, so you can learn how to protect, conserve and amplify your energy in a more magnetic and influential way.
- **Dropping expectations, old stories and 'busy' work that is draining your vibrancy, so you can create more intentional results and attract your people with ease.**
- Connecting with and harnessing your intuitive power, feminine energy, and inner belief to show up for yourself and others without feeling overwhelmed or burnt out.
- **Creating the foundations for how you want to show up for yourself and others that reflects the woman, mother and business owner you desire to be so you can bring it into reality.**

Embody - Stop turning outward for the answers and start being self-guided

- Feeling safe and at home in your body and mind via grounding and mindfulness practices to disconnect from past and future influences impacting your results.
- **Processing challenging thoughts, emotions and behaviours, so you can rewrite your narratives and attract more desirable results and outcomes with ease.**
- Incorporating restorative habits like meditation, affirma-

tions, journalling, and dance to embody more empowering thoughts and supercharge your intuition.
- **Stepping into You 2.0—going all in on your dreams with full self trust, belief and confidence that magnetizes your dream interactions with clients, partners, children and others.**
- Releasing the need to overgive to others and focus on giving to yourself in ways that create less pressure, overwhelm and exhaustion.

Phase 2 - Visibility

Environment - Create an ideal environment that breeds fast results

- Enhancing your internal environment to better support yourself to take inspired action consistently—self-love, intuition, confidence and belief.
- **Implementing morning routines, rituals and habits that support you to energetically align with your goals and achieve them from a place of overflow.**
- Surrounding yourself with positive influences, supportive structures and clear boundaries to show up as the best version of yourself.
- **Stripping back your schedule so you can achieve more by doing less and evoke more joy and calm into your week.**
- Bringing more play and pleasure into your schedule so you can live with more flow, ease and intention.
- **Upleveling your physical environment to support deep**

work that elicits bigger results and reflects your next level and future self.

Empower - Stop feeling forced and start showing up in a way that is powerful and magnetic

- Identifying what it looks like to be your most powerful self and access your divine power, so you can shine your light brighter.
- **Getting crystal clear on exactly what you want in your business and life, so you can open up to call it in and receive it.**
- Getting clear on the worthiness of your why, that you are deserving of your desires and surrendering to the process.
- **Embracing vulnerability and sharing yourself openly—speaking your truth to go from powerless to powerful.**
- Becoming a magnetic, radiant, abundant woman—knowing what makes you magnetic and special so you can share it confidently with the world.
- **Living in connection to your inner truth, becoming self-guided and releasing your need for outside confirmation to start.**

Phase 3 - Impact

Expand - Open up to receive your desires and attract aligned clients with ease

- Believing in the value that you can share and creating offers that feel aligned for you and your audience, so you can create a purposeful income.
- **Embracing your unique energy, story and gifts to create a brand that allows you to stand out and be seen—for being you.**
- Initiating collaborations, leveraging connections and building a loyal audience that allows you to be recognised for your offers and sign clients effortlessly.
- **Working with clients in a way that gets them results, so you can receive raving testimonials and lifelong fans.**
- Raising your standards and opening up to receive more love, money and acceptance from others.
- **Asking for what you want and need in more constructive ways, so you can enforce your new reality and have others respect and support your big vision.**

Elevate - Scale your impact and income with a consistent, automated approach

- Creating abundance through a balance of energy and action, where doing less in a more intentional way yields bigger results.
- **Scaling your brand to impact more people, where you can make money without even being on the clock and focus on living your dream lifestyle.**
- Leveraging automations and more passive offers so you're

able to generate an income while spending time on the things that matter most to you.
- **Leaning on a consistent content schedule and sales funnel that allows you to step back and work on your business rather than in your business.**
- Becoming the CEO of your business and life, where you focus your attention solely on what brings you bliss and empower others to support you in the less blissful things.

If you'd like my personalised support to create and implement your own unique Business Alignment Plan using my signature Intuitive Impact Approach, you can join my Intuitive Impact immersion program or private coaching package that guide you through implementing all of the above and expanding your inner capacity to hold it all – with different levels of coaching support.

Together we'll work on uncovering what's keeping you stuck, how you can show up more intuitively for yourself and your business, and attract the impact you deserve. You'll find website links to these service offerings at the end of the book.

12

Intuitive Impact

'If not this, then what?' I thought.

As I mentioned over the last few chapters, I had a decision to make—revamp my focus and offerings to feel more aligned, or walk away to do something else. Since my miscarriage, I wasn't showing up as my best self and the experience cracked me open to the realisation that things weren't working. After the year that brought us COVID-19, there was a lot of hope and energy around making 2021 better, but I was initially afraid of what that would require and if I could follow through.

I knew that I wasn't ready to walk away from the brand I had been building over the last few years, but I knew that I wasn't aligned with how it was currently positioned and the pressures of how it needed to 'look'. For me to have my true intuitive impact, there needed to be changes across my business and life so I could step into the next level and that's where my Business Alignment Plan became so crucial. Within just a couple of weeks of doing the work, it supported me to manifest my biggest desire of all—becoming a mother!

One of my main values in life is being able to support others to reach their optimal potential and is obviously what attracted me to becoming a counsellor and coach. I knew that if I wasn't doing this work I would be miserable (cue: second quarter-life crisis) so the only option was to forge on with my path and grow along the journey. *'If not this, then what?!'* I thought. This work felt like my only option and my one true calling.

It wasn't easy to discard months of work and things that on the outside were 'working.' But I knew that in order to open up to what could be and have my own intuitively driven impact, I had to let go of what had been and step into what I was being called to.

Now almost mid-way through the year, I'm in the chapter of my life where I'm stepping out of the mushy cocoon and re-emerging as the butterfly—the mother, the aligned entrepreneur, the author. I'm so excited for the next phase of my journey and so grateful to have you following along. The reason that I get to do this work and share myself in this way, is because of people like you who are ready to go within and do the work to bring your desires into reality. I hope that by the time you get to this chapter, you're also in your own process of metamorphosis.

My impact is more than just business focused...it's life focused. I want to have an intuitive impact on my future child, I want to have an intuitive impact on myself, I want to have an intuitive impact on those around me and I want to have an intuitive impact on my audience so they can then go on to have their own intuitive impact.

When we step into our authentic self and create from the

inside out so that we are intuitively driven, we create a ripple effect that positively supports not only those directly in front of us but even the people we don't see and the generations to come.

There's Always Room at the Top

Something that always stood out to me is the notion that there's always room at the top. When you really think about it, so many people never allow themselves to step into their full potential. Many people have the idea or dream in their head, but never take the action to make it a reality. They unfortunately die with undiscovered dreams or opportunities because they chose to take the safe route through life.

Others take the steps to realise their dreams by making the leap into the unknown world of starting a business, but for whatever reason they end up letting things fizzle as they remain snuggled up in their comfort zone. As you continue to climb the mountain towards your goals, you'll notice that more and more people drop off from the journey. They give up, doubt their abilities, take a hiatus, or turn around and retreat back down to where they started. It's those who continue to climb, to persevere and believe, that reach the top of the mountain and find themselves in a space that not many others have conquered.

Think of the mountain as your business. The more you keep moving forward and believe in your ability to reach the heights that you desire, the more and more space there is for you to claim it. If you were to turn around half way when things get challenging and give up on your dreams, then it can mean living with unfulfilled goals.

Being truly valued for who you are and having an impact in the world with your gifts, means allowing yourself to be seen. It means doing the things that many others aren't willing to do. This doesn't mean grinding yourself to the bone with hours of work, or sacrificing parts of your life for your business, but it can mean being innovative or consistent where others are not. It might mean thinking outside the square of how you can present yourself and your content, it might mean going all in on a new platform or new way of sharing content, it might mean providing a product/service in a way that hasn't been done, it might mean embracing who you are—warts and all so that people can really see you.

So next time you feel like quitting and going to work at a local cafe (been there myself), or something happens that makes you feel anything less than the superstar that you are, remind yourself that there's always room at the top. That every step forward, and every step beyond those next to you, takes you further up that mountain and further into spaces where you can shine your light in a bigger way.

Your ABCs

Sometimes it's not enough just to want something. We all want to belong, to be appreciated, to make a difference and to support ourselves financially. But the gap between wanting something and having it is your ABCs.

Action, belief and consistency.

You might think that belief needs to come before action.

But oftentimes, people don't have a bucketload of belief in themselves or the results *until* they start taking action. Think about climbing a mountain again...you might be hopeful that you can achieve the goal of climbing to the top, but you don't *fully* believe it's possible until you start taking the steps and gain confidence the higher you go.

The same is true in business. You may have goals, ideas and dreams that you want to achieve but oftentimes you need to start taking action steps to show yourself that you've got what it takes to put pen to paper and make things happen. As you take more and more action, your belief in your ability continues to strengthen. Sometimes we really do need to 'see' to 'believe.'

A great example of this in my own business is with the Wellbeing Weekly Podcast. When I first decided to start my podcast, I had a certain level of belief in myself. I knew that I would be capable of learning how to record and edit episodes, master the technology, and market myself. But when I first started recording episodes, I couldn't hit record without a script infront of me. I was afraid of making mistakes and sounding like I wasn't making sense...however, the ironic thing about that is when I listen back to those episodes now, I can hear how robotic I sounded. It wasn't until I was taking more and more action by publishing weekly episodes, that my confidence and belief in myself grew. I started recording episodes with just some dot points or talking points and filled the rest in by talking from the heart. To now, one hundred and seventy episodes later, I can hit record and do a whole episode off the top of my head without any fear or anxiety. This is how belief and confidence grow as you keep taking action, *and* it's also where consistency plays a huge part.

If you don't continue to take *consistent* action, then it becomes harder to build your belief and confidence. You begin to build a brand that is flakey—where you show up in bursts and then disappear for weeks or months. It becomes really hard for people to connect with you and trust that you're going to stick around, which then means your results aren't as positive and your belief wavers. This is the point where many can give up completely.

When you're aligned with your 'why' in business, it becomes easier to take consistent action. My why has changed slightly over the years, but my primary motivation with building this brand was to be able to start a family and continue to have an impact and income from work that I enjoyed, while also being present with our children. That vision is now set to become a reality for me come November. So what's your why? What makes you get out of bed every day and show up for your business? What does it allow you to have or create in your life? How can you take consistent action towards it and build your belief daily?

What To Expect When You're 'Not' Expecting

After I told my mum that I was pregnant with our sweet little rainbow baby, she bought me the book *What To Expect When You're Expecting*—the bible to all things pregnancy and childbirth. Pages and pages of everything I could expect each week, each month and throughout labour. But it got me thinking about expectations and how having big expectations on how things in business and life are going to unfold can often be detrimental. If something were to happen differently to what the book said I should 'expect,' how would that feel? Would I think there was something 'wrong' with me or that I wasn't doing pregnancy 'right,' like we begin to think when our expectations elude us?

Expectations refer to having a strong belief that something will happen. We create expectations consciously through our goals and susconciously through the media, society or our upbringing. Based on the law of averages, we often have a pretty good idea of how certain things will turn out for us and we come to expect those results.

But when your expectations don't show up how you want them to, it can leave you feeling rejected, ashamed, defeated and unseen. It can feel like all of your hard work was a waste of time or all of your hopes and dreams were silly and unrealistic. Worst of all, it can make you feel like you're not capable of creating the things that you want and maybe giving up on them altogether. I know the pain and shame that can come with unmet expectations. As a planner, visionary and recovering perfectionist, I've had my fair share of things fall through or not show up for me. But those moments are always a reminder for me to reaffirm that I am on the right path. I just need to redirect slightly and let go of the grip on controlling how the journey unfolds.

So what if you flipped your expectations on their head and had *no* expectations? What could you expect then? You could move through your business and life with a sense of freedom, flexibility and non-attachment to the outcomes. You could set the intentions and release yourself to receive whatever it is that comes your way. Sometimes your set expectations might even be putting limits on what you can receive because you can't yet conceptualise what is possible for you. By dropping the expectations you can open yourself up to things coming into your life in a way you couldn't have possibly dreamt up.

So as you make moves to embody your intuitively driven impact in business and life, I ask you to consider what it would feel like to drop the expectations that things have to reveal themselves or show up in certain ways. Like I mentioned earlier in this book, when you focus your attention and efforts on the what and the why— the how will reveal itself.

Opening Up to Be More and Receive More

What are the people like that you find impactful? Maybe they're scientists, activists, celebrities, teachers, influencers, creatives or even every day people in your life. What is it that they possess or demonstrate that allows them to have an impact on you and others? Oftentimes it can be a simple belief that they can help others with their skills and have a message worthy of sharing. They become open to being a vessel of sharing truth or entertainment or lessons with the world, and in turn allow themselves to receive the accolades of their impact, whether it be praise, money, fame, admiration or love.

In a similar way, in order for you to be impactful within your business you also need to be able to open yourself up to being more than the version you are now and also opening up to receive what may come from that. If you're not ready to step into the next level of your capabilities, or closed off from feeling worthy of the money and exposure that could come your way, then it won't eventuate. You can only receive the things that you believe you can manage.

Now we're not talking about needing to be open to hundreds of thousands of followers or millions of dollars coming your way (unless you want that), but being open to the next level of you and your business. The next level that feels within reach but also a little uncomfortable so that you know you're stretching beyond your comfort zone. What does this next level look like for you? Who do you want to finally give yourself permission to be, and what do you want to give yourself permission to receive? Because you are worthy of it all, when you believe it to be so. And nobody can do that belief work for you.

Rising Up

I've always had a fear of being seen and being judged for trying to show up as myself. I had an anxious mix of not wanting to been seen too much, but also not wanting to be completely ignored or insignificant. It's been a fear that I've consistently pushed through bit by bit throughout the evolution of my identity and businesses. Before my personal brand, I was able to hide in the shadows. I rarely told anyone about my skincare business and very few in my life actually knew how successful it was. I was afraid to stand in my power and be proud of the things I knew and had achieved. But with a personal brand, you *are* the business and there's no hiding because people are paying for *you*.

I've become more and more comfortable being seen and sharing my voice over the years, but it didn't happen all at once. The reason I chose not to use my name as the business was because I didn't feel confident enough to put my name to the brand. I wouldn't even share my name as the author of my podcast episodes. And now, a few years later, I'm putting my name on the front of a book that shares my vulnerable soul journey and am able to step into a much bigger stage for myself and own my name now as my personal brand. Goodbye hiding behind 'brand names'.

But that has come from an amalgamation of tiny leaps of faith...of posting selfies, recording my thoughts on video, doing podcast interviews, coaching clients, and allowing myself to dream bigger and bigger as my confidence surges.

Maybe you're at the beginning of your journey and struggling with the confidence to put yourself out there like I was. That's okay. It's about meeting yourself where you're at and taking that next tiny leap that you can be comfortable with. Sooner or later, posting photos or videos of yourself becomes second nature, marketing yourself becomes enjoyable and you begin to foster a community and audience who value the impact that you can offer them.

Rising up doesn't mean going from A to Z overnight. It means pushing through fear to share yourself in a way that feels aligned to you and taking micro risks to elevate yourself and your brand each day. That's when you can look back in years to come and see how far you've come and how you've allowed yourself to rise up and claim your dreams.

Stepping Into the Arena

You can't have an impact on others, if you don't first put yourself out there in an impactful way. As Brene Brown (Author and Vulnerability/Shame Expert) says, we need to step into the arena and expose ourselves fully to the onlookers in order to rise above and become the influencer. It's easy to sit in the stands and judge others for attempts to better themselves, but how are you showing bravery to step into the arena in your own business and life?

Often people say that if you're jealous or judgemental of others, it's usually a reflection of something you lack in yourself or something you know is possible for you. For example, perhaps you laugh to yourself judgmentally when you see someone sharing a video of themselves online, when really you know that is something you'd like to do within your business but have let fear hold you back—so you mock others to appease yourself.

I believe that there is merit in this notion. I know for myself when I find myself being judgemental or critical of someone, it's often something that I would like to have or something that I've been procrastinating on and not bringing to life for myself. I'm aware when it happens, and it acts as a reminder to take action in this area or to do some work around what is blocking me.

When you step into the arena and allow yourself to be seen in a bigger way, it can be terrifying. You're no longer able to hide in the crowd, or be like everyone else. It's your time to craft your image, demonstrate your confidence and belief, and shine your light to show others what it is you can offer them. It of course opens you up to the potential for criticism, judgement and embarrassment, but that becomes a bargain with yourself over what's more important to you—maintaining anonymity and protecting your ego or showing up as your true self and making a difference to someone out in the crowd?

I remember when I first started my podcast and I said to my partner Chris: *'I'm not going to let a handful of people hold me back from helping thousands of people.'*

I knew I could take the judgement or criticism of people who 'weren't my people' (and really that says more about them than me) so that I could show up and serve the people out there who *wanted* to be impacted by me. And the interesting thing that happened is that I didn't cop any of the nasty criticism or embarrassment that I expected. I actually received the opposite—people supporting me and thinking what I was doing was fantastic. Sometimes, well most of the time, fear tells us lies. So I always say to myself and to my clients, 'You'll never know unless you try—the results might surprise you.'

My Intuitive Impact

As I was coming into the end of writing this book and reflecting on the process of my own re-alignment and what felt most intuitive. I realised one of the biggest ways I had been protecting myself was hiding behind the brand name Wellbeing Weekly. So much has shifted since I first started my podcast and coaching, and as I've shifted more to focusing on offering what feels most intuitive to me and helping other women to do the same - it was only natural that there was one more change to make...

Owning my name.

And so, I made the decision to back myself as the core of my brand and business...that the impact I was having was because of **me**. And my business should reflect that moving forward.

So as I committed to putting my name on the front of this book and declaring myself a published author, I also shifted to Michelle Kerr Coaching. *Ready for the next era of impact.*

Pain, Pleasure, Play, Power, Purpose, Potential

Life is full of P words. Many that we will experience on a regular, if not a daily basis. Some that we need to intentionally harness and incorporate into our days. Remember that you are strong, you are meant to be here, and you are meant to shine your light.

We all have moments of pain and pleasure, it's inevitable as we ride the wave of life...but we get to choose how to infuse play and power into our lives. And ultimately how we live out our purpose and full potential. It's all there within you, and ready to be shared.

— — —

As I rise up into my next phase of business & life, I hope to also inspire you to rise up with me. To claim the space that is yours and create your own intuitively driven impact.

As I share my voice and stories, I hope that you feel confident and empowered to share yourself with the world.

As I shine my light, I hope that you're also ready to shine your light in the brightest way.

Because the world needs your light. The world needs what you have to offer.

There's someone out there right now, waiting for you to cross their paths.

— — —

Thank you from the bottom of my heart for choosing to read this book and make the steps to unlock more of your inner power.

If after reading this book you just *know* I'm the coach for you and you're ready to dive right into expanding your inner capacity and creating more impact, purpose & intention in your career and home - click here or visit:

www.michellekerr.com.au
www.instagram.com/michelle.kerr

13

BONUS: Business Energy Archetype Quiz

This is a short quiz to help you to identify your dominant Business Energy Archetype discussed throughout this book. Keep a tally of your answers and the letter that you select most frequently will align to your most common archetype. You may have a split between two types.

Question 1:

BONUS: BUSINESS ENERGY ARCHETYPE QUIZ

You've been contacted about an opportunity to collaborate on a workshop with a like-minded business. What's your first thought?

A: When do we start?!
B: I hope they vibe with my way of doing things
C: Does this feel good to me?
D: I have so many ideas for content already!
E: As long as I can share my story to inspire others

Question 2:

Which emoji best describes you?

A: 👶💻 Hard Working
B: Innovative
C: ✧ Self Aware:
D: 👶🎨 Talented / Artistic
E: ♀ Strong / Resilient

Question 3:

When it comes to challenges in your business, what would you say is your biggest struggle?

A: Switching off from "doing all the things"
B: Following the strict rules/steps/suggestions of gurus and coaches on how to grow your business
C: Trusting and believing in your own decisions/capability without being swayed or influenced by others
D: Marketing and selling yourself or your work, when you'd rather be working on creating things behind the scenes
E: Opening up and sharing yourself in a vulnerable way. Allowing yourself to be seen authentically - flaws and all

Question 4:

What hobby/activity are you most drawn to?

A: Who has time for hobbies?
B: Sky Diving
C: Yoga Class / Woman's Circle
D: A Pottery Class
E: Reading a Personal Development Book

Question 5:

When it comes to your business, which of the following do you value most?

A: Resilience
B: Individuality
C: Authenticity
D: Creativity
E: Inspiration

Question 6:

In what environment/situation do you do your best work?

A: When you schedule long days or late nights where you can punch out the bulk of your work quickly
B: When you can work on your own and have full ability to define the rules
C: When you have no outside distractions are are able to tune inward to turn your ideas into reality
D: When you have plenty of time and space to think clearly and make decisions that truly express yourself
E: When you have a space that feels comfortable with regular breaks for self care and connecting with others

Question 7:

Which Disney character describes your business situation?

A: Princess Tiana - Working hard to make your business dreams a reality, with little time for rest or fun
B: Ariel - You love to explore new things and pave your own way. You don't care for rules & follow your heart
C: Pocahontas - Connected to your spirit and have intuitive hits that guide your business
D: Rapunzel - You're full of artistic and creative skills/ideas that you love to showcase in your business
E: Mulan - Experienced past adversity / loss and rising up to share your story and support others

Question 8:

In an ideal world, how would you love to spend the majority of time in your business?

A: Marketing and growth strategies to have more income/impactMarketing and growth strategies to have more income/impact
B: Doing whatever you like, whenever you like and not having to answer to anybody about doing things your wayDoing whatever you like, whenever you like and not having to answer to anybody about doing things your way

C: Connecting to your inner world and taking aligned and intuitive action based on the messages you receive

D: Getting lost in the creation of things - whether it's content ideas, website design, podcasting or selling your artistic skills / creations

E: Sharing your story with as many people as possible and providing them with a source of inspiration + support to overcome their own odds

Question 9:

Which beverage sums up the energy/vibe of you and your business?

A: A Strong Coffee
B: Energy Drink
C: Herbal Tea
D: Kombucha
E: Anything Alcoholic

* * *

Results

Mostly A's: The Hustler

Determined. Passionate. Hard Working.
As a hustler energy type, you're a natural go-getter and have always been known for your strong work ethic and ability to make your goals a reality. When you decide on something in your business, you're quick to take action and get it done. People admire you for the consistent progress you make and the dedication you have to creating your desired results.

Unfortunately that can often mean that you neglect other aspects of your life such as self care, relationships or fun. You may find yourself in periods of burnout after prolonged work output and require periods of rest or re-evaluation as you realise that you've over extended yourself.

Aligning your business with this energy:

You're self motivated and rarely run out of energy when it comes to working on what you're passionate about. Having a clear vision & goals will help you to make both a reality. Be mindful of pacing yourself and creating time for other areas of your life to avoid burnout.

Struggle:

Being so work focused that you neglect self care and other areas of your life, often resulting in burn out.

Strength:

Rarely running out of energy & an unwavering belief in making your desired results manifest.

Affirmation:
"Everyday I am closer to my goals"

Value:
Daily personal and professional growth with a never give up attitude

To get further support around honouring and amplifying your Business Energy Archetype for a more aligned impact at work and home, come and join me inside one of my private or group coaching programs

Mostly B's: The Rebel

Individual. Opinionated. Innovative.

As a rebel energy type, you like to do things your way and find it difficult to follow specific rules, steps or pathways instilled by marketing gurus or celebrity entrepreneurs. You believe there a multiple ways to reach your goals and that there is no set criteria that you need to follow, other than listening to your own gut.

You prefer to position yourself as an outlier who does things differently in business and life, embracing your unique personality and ideas so you can showcase them to the world. You like to experiment and try new things, offer things that other's haven't considered, and blaze your own path to success.

Aligning your business with this energy:

You love to share your unique ideas and quirks as a way to connect with your audience authentically. You're strong minded and rarely succumb to feelings of rejection or doubt from those who don't "get it".

Struggle:

Trying to be so individual and rebellious that your audience can't quite relate to you

Strength:

Coming up with innovative ideas that help you to stand out in your space and not being influenced by "what everyone else is doing"

Affirmation:

"I pave my own way and am abundantly compensated for it"

Value:

Doing things when you want, how you want and not letting others tell you what to do with your vision

To get further support around honouring and amplifying your Business Energy Archetype for a more aligned impact at work and home, come and join me inside one of my private or group

coaching programs

Mostly C's: The Intuitive

Perceptive. Empathetic. Spiritual.

You use your gut and inner voice as your main directive when making decisions in business and life. You're a master at shutting out the judgement, opinions and advice of others and turning inward to decipher what it is that feels best for you. You base your business decisions on what feels good for you and feels like an energetic match.

You're tuned into other people's energies and can often absorb what others are feeling just by being in their presence. This can be both a blessing and a curse, requiring you to be able to detach from energies that aren't yours to hold. When you harness this energy, you're able to lean into fully trusting and believing in your own capability and ideas, releasing into divine timing and flow to bring all of your goals to life.

Aligning your business with this energy:
The most important factor for you is to consciously switch off from outside noise. Downloading freebies, podcasts, and engaging multiple mentors/coaches can deter you from your inner wisdom and lead your business in a direction that doesn't

feel like your own.

Struggle :

Taking on other people's energy or feedback rather than listening into your own intuition and knowing

Strength:

Taking action on intuitive hits that may not make sense in the moment, but allow you to get results by connecting with others authentically

Affirmation:

"I turn inward for the answers and trust what comes forth"

Value:

Creating space to tune into your inner world and connect with others on an authentic soul level

To get further support around honouring and amplifying your Business Energy Archetype for a more aligned impact at work and home, come and join me inside one of my private or group coaching programs

Mostly D's: The Creative

Introspective. Visionary. Artistic.

Your primary motivation in life is creating art in it's many forms and sharing your creative bliss with the world. You may find marketing and selling a challenge, because your priority and energy source comes from being a maker / designer / artist / healer. If you could simply create things and have them sell themselves, you would be in your element. Being in your genius zone fuels your energy and you are easily depleted when you feel forced to undertake tasks that pull you away from your creative pursuits.

You prefer to be recognised for your creations and wait for opportunities to come your way, rather than impose yourself on others - but when not implemented correctly it can lead to scattered income.

You communicate, connect and share yourself through your creations and are fulfilled by knowing that others value you and your work.

Aligning your business with this energy:

Your business needs to be centred around your creative work and sharing your genius zone with theworld. When you are sharing from your heart and inspiring others with your gifts/skills, clients will naturally magnetize to you. Your role in the world is to share beautiful creations and ideas that inspire, guide and uplift those who work with you or invest in your creative work.

Struggle:

Forcing your ideas/creations onto others via unaligned marketing strategies, and not feeling valued or seen for your amazing gifts.

Strength:

Producing unique and innovative ideas/creations/insights that allow you to stand out online and be recognised + compensated for your creative mind.

Affirmation:

"When I share my work simply for the love of it, I am abundantly rewarded"

Value:

Expressing yourself and inspiring others through your creative ideas/designs/insights

To get further support around honouring and amplifying your Business Energy Archetype for a more aligned impact at work and home, come and join me inside one of my private or group coaching programs

Mostly E's: The Warrior

Resilient. Inspirational. Strong.

As a Warrior energy type, you use your story and lived experiences as fuel to guide and support others. You often move through peaks and troughs as you navigate your triggers, yet serve as an inspiration to others who have experienced trauma, discrimination or mental health struggles. Authentically sharing your story fuels your energy, and when you feel like you are hiding your truth or shamed for your beautiful vulnerability it can deplete you.

You provide a source of hope for others to be more than their past, their appearance, their limitations or their inner battles and show the world that by embracing all parts of yourself and sharing vulnerably you can achieve great things.

Aligning your business with this energy:

Your brand and business authority is centred around your story of survival, triumph and inspiration. When you openly share your story - flaws and all, you allow your audience to feel hope, belonging and like they can also find success and fulfillment despite their challenges.

Struggle :

Opening up about your experiences and allowing yourself to be vulnerable in public, which makes you less able to connect with your people

Strength:

Sharing the message in the mess and using your lived experience as fuel to support others with their journeys

Affirmation:

"My story is my superpower and how I shine my light"

Value:

Being a role model, advocate and voice for those who may have experienced hardship, trauma or discrimination

To get further support around honouring and amplifying your Business Energy Archetype for a more aligned impact at work and home, come and join me inside one of my private or group coaching programs